Unequal Thailand

T0345341

Unequal Thailand

ASPECTS OF INCOME, WEALTH AND POWER

Edited by

PASUK PHONGPAICHIT AND CHRIS BAKER

NUS PRESS
SINGAPORE

© Pasuk Phongpaichit and Chris Baker

Published by:

NUS Press
National University of Singapore
AS3-01-02, 3 Arts Link
Singapore 117569
Fax: (65) 6774-0652
E-mail: nusbooks@nus.edu.sg
Website: http://nuspress.nus.edu.sg

ISBN 978-981-4722-00-1 (Paper)

First edition 2016
Reprint 2017

National Library Board, Singapore Cataloguing-in-Publication Data

Unequal Thailand: aspects of income, wealth and power/edited by Pasuk Phongpaichit and Chris Baker. – Singapore: NUS Press, [2016]
pages cm
ISBN: 978-981-4722-00-1 (paperback)

1. Equality – Thailand. 2. Income distribution – Thailand. 3. Equality – Economic aspects – Thailand. 4. Equality – Social aspects – Thailand. 5. Equality – Political aspects – Thailand. 6. Capitalism – Thailand.
I. Phongpaichit, Pasuk, editor. II. Baker, Chris, editor.

HC445
338.9593 — dc23   OCN918066141

Printed by: Markono Print Media Pte Ltd

Contents

List of Tables

List of Figures

Abbreviations

ADB	Asian Development Bank
ASEAN	Association of Southeast Asian Nations
BBC	British Broadcasting Corporation
CMA	Capital Market Academy
CNN	Cable News Network
EGAT	Electricity Generating Authority of Thailand
EPMC	Energy Policy Management Committee
EPPO	Energy Policy and Planning Office
ESCS	Economic, Social and Cultural Status
GDP	gross domestic product
IEAT	Industrial Estate Authority of Thailand
IMF	International Monetary Fund
KPI	King Prajadhipok Institute
LTF	Long-term Equity Fund
MP	member of parliament
MoF	Ministry of Finance
NEB	National Environment Board
NEPC	National Energy Policy Council
NESDB	National Economic and Social Development Board
NGO	non-governmental organization
NSO	National Statistical Office
OECD	Organisation for Economic Cooperation and Development
OTOP	One Tambon One Product
PDPC	Power Development Plan Committee
PISA	Programme for International Assessment
PTT	Petroleum Authority of Thailand
PTTEP	PTT Exploration and Production
RMF	Retirement Mutual Fund

SEC   Securities and Exchange Commission
SET   Stock Exchange of Thailand
SOE   state-owned enterprise
TDRI   Thailand Development Research Institute
TEPCoT   Top Executive Program in Commerce and Trade
UDD   United Front for Democracy against Dictatorship
UNDP   United Nations Development Programme

Preface

What makes a society more unequal, what are the consequences, and what could or should be done about it—these are issues that are complex and controversial. This book has the modest aim of offering some new data and new thinking from a country where inequality has become a problem.

This project began with some brainstorming sessions. Outside, Bangkok's streets were filled with demonstrators, dressed in contrasting colors and offering starkly contrasting views on how the country should be run. The researchers we gathered came from academia, government service, the private sector, and the activist community. Their expertise spanned economics, politics, agriculture, taxation, and finance. For thought starters, we had talks from Ammar Siamwalla, a macroeconomist, and Ben Anderson, a historian. We urged each of the researchers to use their particular expertise and experience to bring something new to the debate on inequality.

In this book, we present a selection of the output from the project, selecting the work that fulfilled the aim of contributing "something new" in different ways. In some cases, that is new data. Duangmanee Laovakul presents the first national analysis of the distribution of land based on ownership documents. To generate these data, she had to persuade the Land Department to allow access to their database for the first time, and get special software written for the analysis. In some cases, the researchers have opened up new subjects of study. Nopanun Wannathepsakul shows how an unusual blend of public and private enterprise lies behind both the upside and downside of Thailand's booming energy sector. Nualnoi Treerat and Parkpume Vanichaka open a window onto the informal elite networking that is invisible to conventional political research and analysis. Some of the studies use sophisticated tools. While several studies have shown how education contributes to Thailand's extreme inequalities, here Dilaka Lathapipat uses econometrics to identify the critical areas in need of reform. Some offer new approaches to the practical questions of reform. Sarinee Achavanuntakul's team shows how the stock market contributes to economic inequalities, and draws on international experience to suggest how that can be overcome. Pan Ananapibut presents proposals for overhauling Thailand's antiquated and patently unfair tax systems. Some take a new look at more conventional areas of study. Chaiyon Praditsil and Chainarong Khrueanuan add a new chapter to the study of godfathers in local politics. Ukrist Pathmanand examines how political networks are constructed at the national level.

In the opening chapter, we offer a general overview of the interplay between economic and political factors in Thailand's inequality. Over the "development era," inequality in incomes grew exceptionally wide, and has moderated only partially in the last few years. A result, which has been poorly appreciated until new data appeared only recently, has been the development of even starker inequality in the distribution of wealth.

While inequalities of both income and wealth can be explained in terms of economic mechanisms, these mechanisms operate within a political context which also needs to be understood. We argue that a useful concept for understanding Thai politics is oligarchy, rule of the few. This operates in different ways and at different levels. Because of a generally low degree of institutionalization in Thai politics, informal networks and coalitions of the few play major roles in the distribution of power and economic benefits, as illustrated here in the chapters by Ukrist, Nualnoi, and Chaiyon and Chainarong. In some cases, institutions are shaped to protect or promote the privileges of the few, as the chapters by Sarinee's team and Nopanun show. Often these formal and informal mechanisms of oligarchy show extraordinary flexibility in preserving privilege in the face of challenge and change, as discussed in the chapters by Ukrist, and Chaiyon and Chainarong.

Overall, oligarchy survives because it is not successfully challenged. Moving Thailand towards a more equal and peaceable society will not be easy or quick. The reforms that are needed in areas such as taxation, budgeting, finance, and education are not difficult to identify, and indeed have been known for years, but remain undone because the political will is not there, or, to phrase that differently, because oligarchy rules.

The chapters were produced under a three-year project titled "Towards a More Equitable Thailand: A Study of Wealth, Power, and Reform." All the studies here were originally written in Thai, mostly as research reports of 100–150 pages, and some are posted at http://www.econ.chula.ac.th/research/project?topic=Poli_Topic. These were shortened to become chapters in the Thai-language book, *Su sangkom thai samoe na* [Towards a More Equitable Thailand], edited by Pasuk and published by Matichon in 2014. Here we have adapted the chapters into English, and often shortened them still further.

We are very grateful to the Thailand Research Fund, the Bureau of Higher Education and Chulalongkorn University who jointly financed the research for this project under the Distinguished Professor Scheme.

We are indebted to the Land Department of the Ministry of Interior who allowed access to their database on *chanot* land documents for the first time.

We would like to thank the Center for Southeast Asian Studies at Kyoto University, and especially Professor Kaoru Sugihara. We are grateful to Kobsak Pootrakool for permission to reuse his charts.

We thank other members of the research group, not represented in the book, including Nuarpear Lekfuangfu, Khemmarat Thalerngsi, Sithidej Pongkitvorasin, Thanee Chaiwat and Sathaporn Roengtham. We owe thanks to those who helped the group as critics, reviewers and consultants including Ammar Siamwalla, Ben Anderson, Anan Kanjanaphan, Medhi Krongkaew, Precha Piempongsant, and Chatthip Nartsupha. We are grateful to two readers of NUS Press for very cogent advice.

We owe a special debt to Chairat Sangaroon, our legal advisor, who read everything very carefully. On his advice, we have had to refrain from revealing the personal names of some sources of information and some persons mentioned in the text.

Pasuk Phongpaichit
Chris Baker
Bangkok, April 2015

1

Introduction:
Inequality and Oligarchy

PASUK PHONGPAICHIT AND CHRIS BAKER

With rapid growth from the 1960s onwards, inequality in income in Thailand grew sharply worse. Over the past 15 years, this situation has eased slightly, but Thailand is still one of the most unequal societies in Asia. As those at the top of the income pyramid have saved more, inequality in wealth is even more skewed, especially in ownership of land and financial assets. These economic inequalities underlie inequalities of power, social position and access to resources of all kinds. Power is concentrated in the hands of the few at the top of the economic pyramid. This principle of oligarchy is found not only in national politics but also in institutions and structures throughout society. These inequities lie behind Thailand's political turmoil of recent years. People do not resent economic inequalities directly so much as inequalities in access to power and resources such as good education, a fair trial, and a decent chance in life. These resentments are clearly present in the political rhetoric of the Red camp. At the same time, Yellow rhetoric articulates fears that democratic processes will threaten the current pattern of privilege. Government policies of taxation and spending can contribute to easing inequality. Other countries have shown how. Thailand needs to increase the supply of public goods such as good education, health care, public transport, uncorrupt policemen and fair judges. Because income and wealth are so skewed, this can be financed at little social cost by tightening the administration of personal income tax and introducing new taxes on wealth. Other reforms are needed to undo monopolies and other privileges. All this is easy to see, but hard to do. Social pressure will be needed to overcome oligarchy, but the benefits will be a fairer, more peaceable, and more successful society. In one paragraph, this is the argument of this book.

In a recent article, Kevin Hewison (2015) has underlined the extent to which inequality pervades Thailand's economy, society and culture.

> Thailand's inequality has a prodigious influence and exercises the whole course of society, by giving a certain direction to state ideology and a particular tenor to the laws by imparting maxims to the governing powers, and habits to the governed. The influence of inequality extends beyond politics and law: it creates opinions, engenders sentiments, suggests the ordinary practices of life, and modifies whatever it does not produce. The inequality of conditions in Thailand is the fundamental fact from which all others are derived.

All over the world there has been concern over inequality in recent years. Growing disparities of income and wealth are widely seen as a major legacy of the neoliberal era and its faith in market against government. Recent years have also seen an upward trend in political instability with clashes in many European cities and growing turmoil across the Islamic world. Economists once argued that inequality contributed to growth by motivating people to improve themselves. Now they are more likely to argue that inequality underlies the political conflict that disrupts long-term growth (Berg et al. 2008).

Around 20 years ago, we wondered aloud whether the rapidly widening income gap in Thailand would have social and political consequences. Colleagues were generally dismissive of this concern. Inequality is a natural thing, some argued, and economic growth was the priority; inequality would either be solved eventually by trickle-down, or could be addressed by policy at a later date. In recent years, this complacency has dissolved. The reason is the persistent turmoil of Thai politics over the past decade. The goal of reducing inequality is now written into the national plan, analyzed in reports of leading think tanks, and appeared on the agenda of the 2014 coup junta. Writers of the 2015 constitution explained their approach by stating, "disparity in income, wealth distribution, and access to opportunities constitutes the underlying root cause of the social and economic ills of the nation" (Bowornsak and Navin 2015: 4).

The first section of this chapter sets the issue of inequality in Thailand into the international context of concern over growing inequality and its impact on political stability and economic growth. The second summarizes the trends of economic inequality in Thailand, highlighting the rapid growth of an income gap in the development era, the limited reduction of the gap over the past two decades, and the high level of wealth inequality revealed by recent data. The third section discusses the relationship between economic inequality and the political conflict of the past decade. The fourth examines the oligarchic tendencies in Thai politics that help to sustain inequality into the future. The fifth suggests some basic reforms to move Thailand towards a fairer and more peaceable society.

Inequality in an International Perspective

The year 2014 was the year of inequality. In January, the UN Development Programme (UNDP) published a major report on *Humanity Divided: Confronting Inequality in Developing Countries*; in February, the International Monetary Fund (IMF) published a note on *Redistribution, Inequality and Growth*, and the head of the IMF said that rising inequality casts a "dark shadow... across the global economy." In April, the Asian Development Bank (ADB) issued a report on *Inequality in Asia and the Pacific*. In December, the Organisation for Economic Cooperation and Development (OECD) issued a report on *Inequality and Growth*. At the start of 2015, the International Labour Office (ILO) issued a book on *Labour Markets, Institutions and Inequality* (Berg 2015). Rarely have the major international organizations converged on one subject in this way. In his State of the Union address, President Barack Obama (2014) noted "Inequality has deepened," and promised to devote 2014 to tackling the issue in the US.[1] Pope Francis tweeted: "Inequality is the root of social evil." Oxfam announced that the richest 1 per cent of the population would own half the world's wealth by 2016. And a 700-page tome, packed with data and written by a French economist, hovered near the top of the New York Times rankings, attracting sell-out audiences on the lecture circuit, and winning acclaim as a major intellectual milestone of a century that has barely started. In just a few months, Piketty's *Capital in the Twenty-First Century* became the Harry Potter of the dismal science.

The build-up had begun a few years earlier. Several studies had documented trends of income concentration in the advanced economies, especially the US. In the financial crisis of 2008, the Occupy Movement popularized the slogans "The One Percent" and "We are the 99 Percent," which gave new political meaning to the inequality issue. Here we will review some major contributions to show the range and complexity of the debate.

Key Contributions to the International Debate

From the US, Joseph Stiglitz (2011, 2012) and James Galbraith (2013) show how the neoliberal policies begun in the Reagan-Thatcher years, especially reducing social welfare spending and deregulating banks and business, led to increased inequalities of income and wealth in the US and in most other advanced economies. They argue that, as a greater proportion of wealth accumulates in the hands of the rich, less is used for productive purposes leading to growth. As credit becomes more and more important in the ability of the rest to survive, banking crises become more and more common. As the gaps of income, wealth and lifestyle separating people in the same society gape ever wider, the sense of community and mutual trust declines. As people become more and more convinced that governments make policies to favor the rich, their faith in democracy weakens, signaled by falling electoral turnouts. Stiglitz's subtitle sums up the fear: *How Today's Divided Society Endangers our Future*. In this analysis, inequality is a threat to future growth, to economic stability, to social cohesion, and to democracy itself.

From the UK, Richard Wilkinson and Kate Pickett's *The Spirit Level* (2009) focuses not on why inequality has worsened, but on what its results are. The authors are not economists, but medics. By comparing statistics from different countries, they claim that more unequal societies have more crime, less trust, more anxiety, more mental and physical health problems, poorer education performance, more violence, and less mobility. Several critics have challenged the data and the methods of analysis, but the book sold in thousands and its argument clearly struck a chord.

In *The Society of Equals* (2013), the French philosopher-historian Pierre Rosanvallon argues that rising inequality reflects shifts in social values. From the 18th century, the "liberty, equality, fraternity" ideology of the French Revolution spread an aspiration for a "society of equals." But since the collapse of socialism on a world scale in the late 20th century, individualism has become the dominant social value, overwhelming any aspiration for social equality, and licensing the destruction of the redistributive state.

Thomas Piketty (2014) argues that there is a "law" in the operation of capitalism leading to greater inequality of wealth. That law is simply that the rate of return to capital (various forms of assets or wealth) is always higher than the overall rate of growth ("r>g"). The current situation of sharply increasing inequality is not the result of neoliberalism or individualism, but the normal state of affairs. The trend towards equality in the 20th century was abnormal, a result of the massive destruction of assets in two world wars. The message is that societies will become more and more unequal unless governments act to counter Piketty's law. He proposes a global tax on financial transactions to fund redistribution.

Several critics have pointed out that Piketty's "law" is just an observation on the data, with no explanation of the mechanisms at work, and that his solution of a global tax is utopian. These critics may be right but also may be missing the point. Piketty's work is a contribution to the politics of policy debate more than a contribution to economic theory. It provides a justification for social democracy, for government intervention in the economy and for spending on social programs. Since the collapse of the world socialist movement in the 1980s, this argument has been under attack. Piketty has been celebrated because he offers a glimmer of theoretical hope for those who regret the decline of social protection and the ethos of a caring and inclusive society ever since the Reagan-Thatcher era. Whereas the "One Percent" slogan focuses resentment against growing inequality, Piketty's "r>g" justifies government actions to do something about it.

In sum, a lot of ink has been spilt on the issue of inequality in the last few years. The participants in the debate include not only economists but also political scientists, medics, historians, and philosophers. Several factors have contributed to this surge of interest, but probably the most important is worry about the decay of social cohesion, and the rise of protest and conflict. Joseph Stiglitz (2011) expresses this worry in the simplest and clearest terms: "It's easier to act together [as a society] where most people are in similar situations", and harder where the social divisions are wide. Talking about the US, he drew attention to "the erosion of our sense of identity, in which fair play, equality of opportunity, and a sense of community are so important."

An Asian Perspective

One striking feature of this literature is that it focuses on the advanced western economies. Among Piketty's many case studies, none are from Asia and none from the developing world. He refers only briefly to China and India. This bias is generally true of this literature as a whole.

But rising inequality is also a feature of Asia and of the developing world. Within ASEAN, inequality has risen in the Philippines, Indonesia, and Laos in recent years (see Figure 1.4 below). In India and China, where socialist-inspired regimes have been supplanted by free-market capitalism, inequality has risen markedly. In both countries, the Gini Index in the early 1990s was around 0.32. By 2010, it had risen to 0.37 in India, and 0.43 in China.

While neoliberalism and Piketty's intrinsic trend of capitalism may indeed contribute to the growing inequality in Asia, other simpler factors also play a role.

In the quest for economic development, governments across the region have promoted entrepreneurial capitalism, tolerated monopolies, suppressed labor activism, failed to protect the environment, and fostered weak judicial regimes. As a result, much business growth has an element of "primitive accumulation," or in modern jargon, free-wheeling rent-seeking and unrestrained exploitation of natural and human resources to create abnormal levels of profit (Khan and Jomo 2000). Many of the leading business figures are self-made men and women who have made spectacular fortunes in a single lifetime. In Thailand, the currently richest man started his working career frying noodles on the pavement. His rapid rise was assisted by monopoly arrangements, tax evasion, access to power, and help from government (Nualnoi 2008). The Forbes rankings of the wealthiest people from other countries are packed with similar figures. *Old money* may be steadily accumulating through Piketty's formula, but *new money* is growing much faster, with help from the powerful.

The rapid urbanization that has come with globalization, and the major investments by government in infrastructure, have boosted the value of property, especially in major cities, but also in the hinterlands. This has brought windfall profits both to traditional landowners and to upcoming developers and speculators.

At the same time, old social ideologies and structures that help to underpin inequality have survived into the modern world. These include caste systems, patron-client relations, monarchy, titled aristo-cracy, and other remnants of *anciens regimes*. Although many recent Asian leaders, including Gandhi and Mao, have promoted an ethic of equality, the region has no equivalent of the European enlighten-ment's assertion of the fundamental equality of man—an ideology that has been accepted as part of the historical inheritance of a whole region. To put it bluntly, the justification of inequality is not unimag-inable in Asia in the same way that it is in the West.

Third, political systems around Asia are marked by oligarchy, rule by the few. This is true of post-socialist regimes and one-party states, but also of nominally democratic regimes, where informal structures and networks operate below the surface. These oligarchies are in part a legacy of the past—of patrimonialism associated with monarchy, military rule, and colonial distortions. But these oligarchies are also a function of inequality, a result of the extreme concentration of econo-mic and political power, as well as a buttress of continuing inequality. They constantly adapt in response to changes in the international and domestic environment, co-opting new selected groups that rise to power, and confronting challenges. These oligarchies embrace patri-monial relationships when it suits them and have an aversion to democratic principles of equality, rule of law and social justice for all.

In sum, neoliberalism and trends within capitalism may contri-bute to rising inequality in Asia, but there are other factors that may be more important, including development policy, old forms of hierarchy, and the persistence of oligarchy and strong conservatism against democratic principles.

Economic Inequality in Thailand

Worsening Inequality of Income in the Development Era

From the 1960s to the 1990s, Thailand became a much less equal society (Figure 1.1). In 1962, at the first calculation based on house-hold survey data, the Gini Index (a measure of income distribution in which a higher figure means greater inequality) was 0.413, around the average for developing countries. Thirty years later it had risen to 0.536, among the highest in the world, surpassed only by some countries in Africa and Latin America.[2] The deterioration had been especially steep from the mid-1980s onwards, the era of breakneck growth fuelled by market liberalization and the inflow of East Asian investment.

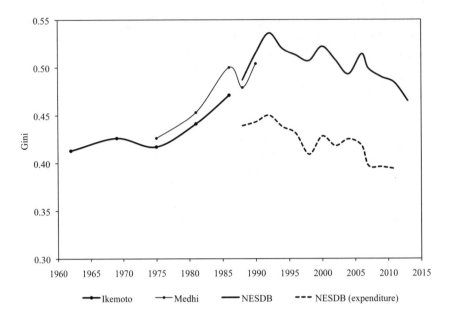

Figure 1.1   Gini Indices, Thailand, 1962–2013

Source: 1981–86, Ikemoto and Uehara (2000: 426); 1988–2011, NSO/NESDB; 2013, unofficial preliminary calculation by a private researcher using NSO data. The Ikemoto and Uehara and NSO/NESDB series roughly coincide for 1988 and 1990.

Many factors contributed to this trend, but four were paramount. First, the government promoted growth by granting favors to capital while repressing labor (Glassman 2004; Jetin 2012). Second, growth was heavily concentrated around Bangkok, and measures to counter this concentration were weak and ineffective. Third, as Thailand was steadily enveloped by globalization, the prices, profits, and salaries for some adjusted towards international levels, and urban property values boomed. Fourth, from the mid-1970s onwards, world agricultural prices fell relentlessly, dragging down farm incomes (Medhi 1993; Ikemoto 1991; Ikemoto and Uehara 2000). Medhi (1993: 435) concluded, "The populations of Bangkok and the Central Region continue to reap the benefits of development, whereas those in the rural areas struggle behind."

Finally, there was no political interest or will to combat growing inequality. It was not seen as a problem, and not raised as an issue in the development plans of the Cold War era. Here neighboring Malaysia provides the telling contrast. The trend of its Gini Index over this era is almost a mirror image of that of Thailand. It started much higher, around the level of Thailand's peak, and ended much lower. Erik Kuhonta (2011) has argued that the racial riots of 1969 convinced Malaysia's leaders that inequality had to be reduced, resulting in policies such as universal health care, land reform, tax changes, and the positive discrimination of the *bumiputera* policy. By contrast, Thai government policies tended to confirm rather than counter inequality. The tax structure, heavily dependent on indirect taxes, weighed more heavily on the poor than the rich, who benefited from copious loopholes. Government spending was concentrated in Bangkok, and later in some large and urbanized provinces whose politicians were deft at capturing funds from the national budget (Warr 2003; Hyun 2009; TDRI 2015).

Gabriel Palma argues that inequality is a reflection of the structural distribution of power in society. At times of rapid economic growth, social and political elites often have the power to grab a disproportionate share for themselves, and at times of crisis, they are often better at defending themselves. From studying income distribution across the world, Palma notes that the middle part of the income pyramid tends to be rather stable across countries and across time. In brief, the "middle 50 per cent" (from the 5th to 9th decile) tend to have a roughly 50 per cent share of total income. Inequality increases when the powerful top 10 per cent is able to increase its share at the expense of the powerless bottom 40 per cent, and decreases when the bottom 40 per cent is able to claw something back. The Palma Ratio, computed by dividing the share of the top 10 per cent by the share of the bottom 40 per cent, is thus a clearer and more sensitive indicator of change in income distribution than the Gini Index (Palma 2011).

Figure 1.2 shows the dramatic change. Over the boom era from 1981 to 1992, the top 10 per cent increased their share of total income by 8 percentage points. In 1981, the top 10 per cent had 2.5 times the income of the bottom 40 per cent. By 1992, this ratio had become almost four times.

The Trend Turns in the 1990s

From a peak of 0.536 in 1992, the Gini Index has been improving to reach 0.484 at the latest official reading from 2011 (and 0.465 in 2013 from preliminary unofficial calculations). The Palma Ratio has

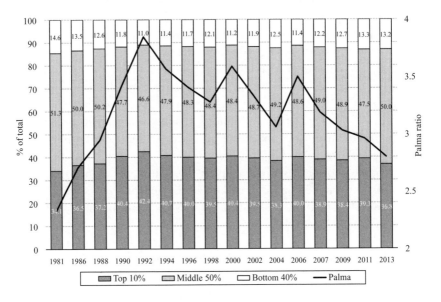

Figure 1.2 Palma Ratio, Thailand, 1981–2013

Source: Own calculation from NSO/NESDB data.

fallen in parallel. The trend has not been steady, but a zigzag, complicated at first by the bubble economy and 1997 financial crisis, so that only recently has the downward trend become clear.

Kobsak Pootrakool (2013) has subjected this trend to a sophisticated statistical analysis. His major finding is that incomes have converged in the middle range of the pyramid (Figure 1.3). If the population is divided into percentiles (1 per cent groups) ranked by income, then those from around 5 to 60 have seen their incomes grow faster than the average over 1988–2011, while those from around 60 to 99 have seen their incomes grow slower than the average.

The occupations where incomes have grown faster than the average include farm owners, tenants and landless workers, as well as general manual workers (Kobsak 2013: 35, chart 18). The gap between urban and rural has narrowed slightly. The regional economies have grown faster than Bangkok, especially since the post-crisis recovery of the early 2000s, and especially in the poorest regions of the south and northeast.

Many factors lie behind this convergence. The issue of inequality became part of the national agenda, first mentioned in the 10th national plan of 2007–11, though with little effect on policy. More

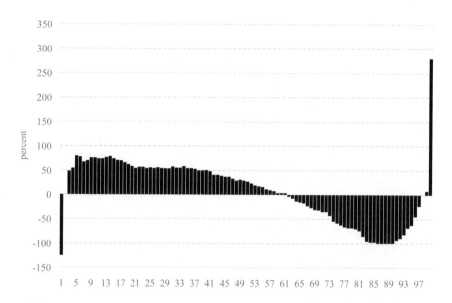

Figure 1.3 Relative Change in Income by Percentile, Thailand, 1988–2011
Source: Kobsak (2013: 37).

importantly, through the mechanisms of parliamentary democracy, politicians have responded to social demands for better public goods and services. The Thaksin government of 2001–05 introduced a universal health care scheme, several windows of microcredit, and additional farm price subsidies. The health care scheme is credited with moving several hundred thousand households above the poverty line by reducing household expenditure on health, and safeguarding poor households against the financial disaster of a health crisis in the family (Nualnoi 2013). The impact of the other measures are more difficult to gauge, but Thaksin was rewarded with high popularity, and people told surveys and interviewers that they gave him loyal support because of the impact of these measures (Naruemon and McCargo 2013: 1015–6).

Second, the initial improvement in the Gini Index came in the bubble before the 1997 crisis when the labor market became tight, and real wages improved. This trend was disrupted by the crisis, but returned in the early 2000s, despite the influence of the in-migration of several million unskilled workers from neighboring countries.

Third, agricultural prices trended upwards in the early 2000s, prompting expansion of cultivation of rubber and fuel crops.

Fourth, the policy of decentralization to elected local government bodies, inaugurated in 1999, resulted in a shift of government budget away from the center, more to the provinces and more to the rural areas. Although local bodies were often criticized for corruption and wasteful spending, they have also responded to constituents' demands by providing better basic services including piped water and paved roads.

Finally, people have not been passive agents in this process of convergence but have moved to tap the unevenly distributed gains of growth. Labor migration began from the early development era, but swelled in the early mid-1990s when around five million persons transferred out of agriculture into industrial and service sector jobs, and continued after the recovery from the 1997 crisis. A large factor in the faster-than-average growth in rural incomes has been the contribution of transfers from family members working in the urban economy.

While the trend towards better income distribution now seems well established, three major problems remain.

First, as Kobsak (2013: 38) shows, while incomes of most of those in the top two-fifths of the income pyramid grew slower than average over 1988–2011, the incomes of the top 1 per cent grew spectacularly fast, around 2.8 times the average. In short, Kobsak has discovered that Thailand has a "1 per cent problem" just like the US and many of the advanced economies. This top 1 per cent group includes 600,000 to 700,000 people in families headed by businessmen, property owners, professionals and managers. As Kobsak (2013: 68–9) notes,

> Households at the top of the pyramid have been favored by the state through concessions, protection against competition, and various privileges which increase the level of rent in the system, because of the connections between these households and those in power resulting in policies and measures which reward, support, and maintain the mutual advantages of both parties...by leveraging these advantages, in the long run they accumulate wealth, riches, property, land and various benefits clearly different from those lower down the pyramid.

Second, as Kobsak also shows, the bottom 1 to 5 per cent of the pyramid miss out on the trend of convergence. Their incomes have grown significantly slower than the average. The households are mostly rural, resident particularly in the northeast, with an older and less educated household head, and larger-than-average household size.

Third, while the spatial factor in income inequality has diminished since 1988, education has become a bigger factor in determining differences in income level. As the economy has grown in sophistication, the income premium for those with secondary and (especially) tertiary education has sharply increased (Dilaka 2013). Over recent decades, the *quantity* of education has increased—enrolment ratios are up, and average years of schooling have lengthened—but the quality of schooling has lagged behind, and is very unevenly distributed. In the international PISA tests of educational quality, Bangkok students perform on par with those in the US, while students from the rural northeast are on par with those from some countries in Africa (Pasuk and Pornthep 2013). Analyzing panel data tracking households across several years, Kobsak (2013: 53, 61) shows that social mobility is still rather limited: those in the bottom fifth of the income pyramid have only a 50 per cent chance of improving their status; those in the middle ranges have an equal chance of going up, down, or standing still; while "the richest can maintain their status rather well." The chances of a child gaining a better education than their household head is still rather low.

Under the "capability approach"[3] to diminishing inequalities, access to education is a key concern. Designing policies to improve access requires detailed analysis of the factors that determine the current inequality. In Chapter 3 of this book, Dilaka Lathapipat shows that the situation of Thai education has changed rapidly over the past two decades. As a result of policy to expand basic education, access to upper secondary education has improved. But at the tertiary level, access has become more unequal, and household wealth has become increasingly important as the determining factor. Dilaka shows that subsidies for tertiary education of the poor will not work on their own. More needs to be done to improve access to good quality education from the pre-school level onwards, especially in poorer regions.

While income distribution in Thailand has improved over the past two decades, it is still high in comparison to countries of a similar income level, and in comparison to its neighbors in ASEAN (see Figure 1.4).[4]

Inequality of Wealth

The capacity to save and to accumulate wealth has been heavily concentrated at the top of the income pyramid. One of Kobsak's most striking findings is that the top 1 per cent derive around 30 per cent

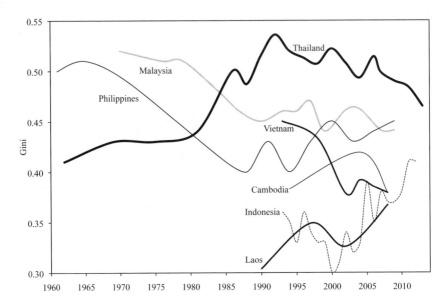

Figure 1.4 Gini Indices for Selected ASEAN Countries, 1962–2013

of their income from investments and rents, while the next highest 5 per cent earn only around 2–3 per cent of their incomes from this source, and the bottom half of the income pyramid gain virtually nothing (Kobsak 2013: 68). In other words, around half of all income from investment and rents is captured by the top 1 per cent of the income pyramid.

The capacity to save, as measured by the gap between income and expenditure, has always been higher in the top income quintile, and this gap has grown much greater over recent decades (Figure 1.5). In the bottom 40 per cent of the income pyramid, many save nothing and fall into debt, while the top 20 per cent commands 80 to 90 per cent of total household savings. This inequity is exaggerated by differences in access to financial services. Over a fifth of rural households have no bank account and many rely on informal moneylenders (Kobsak 2013: 48). Even in the middle-income ranks, few have access to the higher returns from the capital market. Only 330,000 people are active shareholders in the stock exchange (see Chapter 4).

Sustained over a long period, such variation in saving leads to concentration of wealth. Until recently, studies of inequality in Thailand focused on income because no data on wealth were available.

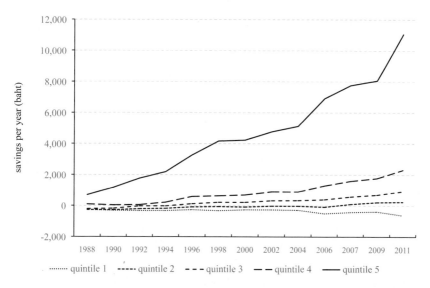

Figure 1.5 Savings (Income minus Expenditure) by Quintile, Thailand, 1988–2011

Source: Kobsak (2013: 68).

That has now changed. Since 2006, the biannual Household Socio-economic Survey by the National Statistical Office (NSO) has covered wealth. These surveys show that distribution of wealth is even more skewed than distribution of income (which is usually the case) with a Gini Index of around 0.7. Strikingly, there is a very big gap between the top 20 per cent and the next 20 per cent, even though we can guess that those at the top are more likely to have concealed their real wealth. There are some problems with these official data, but other sources confirm the pattern. Duangmanee Laovakul has made the first nationwide analysis of land distribution based on land titles, reported in Chapter 2 of this volume. Her study shows a very skewed distribution of land with a Gini Index of a staggering 0.88. The top tenth own 61 per cent of all titled land. The bottom tenth own 0.1 per cent. The biggest landholder has 100,000 hectares. Duangmanee makes a strong case for taxing wealth on grounds of efficiency and equity.

Inequality, Social Conflict and Politics

In the last few years, the refusal to address the issues of income and wealth inequality in Thailand has partially dissolved. Promoting equality now figures in the national plan. The mainstream think tank has made studies and policy proposals (TDRI 2015). Political parties have included the issue in their electoral programs.

In part this shift is a reflection of the international debates outlined above. More significantly, it is a result of Thailand's political conflict of the past decade. Some people (but not all) have realized that inequality lies behind this conflict in some way.

The relationship between inequality, protest and political conflict is rather complex, and controversial. Some people became very upset about social interpretations of the Red-Yellow conflict in Thailand. These people protested against BBC and CNN for portraying the conflict as between poor and rich. Some claimed that Thailand has a special quality as a unified, division-free, class-free society. The junta installed by the 2014 coup forbade discussion of inequality on grounds it would foment social conflict. This does not seem very clever politics. No football team has won a match by claiming the other side does not exist.

Others claim class is an old-fashioned concept, and that the society of today has moved beyond the era of the Cold War. This is true. The conflict of recent years has been rather complex. History, regionalism, personalities, and ideology have all played a part in shaping the political division. But social class surely has a major role.

Figure 1.6, based on a survey of protesters by the Asia Foundation (2013: 7), shows that the income profiles of the Red and Yellow protesters were quite different—the Reds towards the lower end of the income scale and the Yellows to the higher. This was obvious to any observer (see also Naruemon and McCargo 2013; Apichart, Yukti and Niti 2013; Hewison 2015). The Yellow protests were full of Bangkok businesspeople and office workers; the Red ones were drawn from the smallholder farming communities of the provinces, and labor migrants from a similar background.

But this is not class politics in an old sense. Over the past generation, average real incomes in Thailand have multiplied by three. As Apichart, Yukti and Niti (2013) have shown, the core catchment for the Red Shirt movement was not the very poor, but rather those who have been borne up by this prosperity, and are climbing upwards into a "new middle class" or "proto middle class." They have wider horizons and rising expectations, often as a result of their experience of labor migration, both to Thailand's cities and overseas. Studies by Somchai (2012), Walker (2012), Pinkaew (2013) and Keyes (2013)

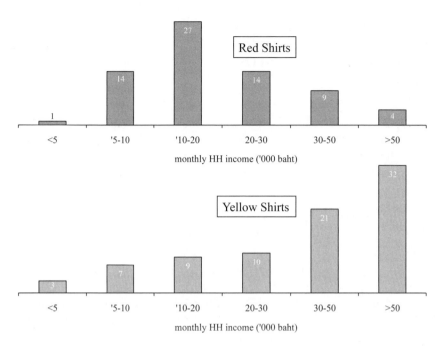

Figure 1.6 Income Profiles of Red and Yellow Protesters, 2013
Source: Asia Foundation (2013: 7).

have come to similar conclusions. Like the upwardly mobile every-where, they dream of becoming rich themselves, and have no resentment against wealth or inequality in themselves. But inequalities of income and wealth, especially extreme inequalities, breed other kinds of inequality which become built into the structure of society and the attitudes of its members. The rich acquire privileged access to power, justice, education, health and other public goods. They believe that this privileged access is a right. The claim to human dignity also becomes unequally distributed within society. Resentments are created when those with new aspirations confront the structures and attitudes founded on economic inequality.

These resentments can be read from the vocabulary and rhetoric of the Red Shirt movement. They railed against *song matrathan*, "double standards," the way that certain groups in the society get treated better than others and think they deserve it. They dubbed themselves as *phrai* and their opponents as *ammat*, words for serf and lord from the old feudal order. This vocabulary brilliantly mocked the assumptions of privilege by the old establishment, and its refusal to recognize that times are changing. In sum, these two phrases revealed a demand to be treated on an *equal* level.

Apichart, Yukti and Niti (2013: 59–60) recount an interview with a protester who

> felt slighted…especially at being looked down upon…by a television presenter saying, 'Isan people can only be servants and petrol pump boys.' He showed his pent-up resentment by saying 'I felt insulted and held in contempt because [such people] think I'm poor, uneducated. I feel society has classes, has problems of inequality, money under the table, connections.

The umbrella organization of the Red Shirts explained, "We want a free capitalist state in which the gap between the rich and the poor is reduced. We want to create more opportunities for the poor." They wanted a "fair and just state," where "the people are free of the aristocratic oligarchy (*ammat*) and have pride, freedom and equality" (quoted in Hewison, 2015). On similar lines, one Red Shirt protester told Claudio Sopranzetti (2012: 12), "What we mean by democracy is fairness…. We want fairness in three ways: legal, political, and educational." Protestors are not only aware of disparity, but also conscious that elections are a mechanism to secure change. Another protestor told an interviewer, "Bangkok people already have a good life, they don't need elections for change, but we do" (Naruemon and McCargo 2013: 1015).

Explaining the need for a program of reform in the 2015 draft constitution, Kobsak Pootrakool, one of the drafters, explained, "If you listen to the protesters, they are saying: this society is not equal, not just, not fair."[5]

As in many middle-income countries, all kinds of public goods are in short supply, not only roads, hospitals, and good schools, but also effective policing and access to judicial process. Anything in short supply tends to be badly distributed, with the rich and powerful grabbing an unfair share. In Bangkok, there is one doctor for every thousand people; in some northeast provinces, it is one per ten thousand (UNDP 2014: 138–9). Some 60 per cent of youths from the top income quartile enroll at college, but only 10 per cent of youths from the bottom quartile, a gap of six times (World Bank 2009: 37).

This rhetoric is not against inequalities of income and wealth as such, but against other inequities that develop in an economically unequal society, especially the unfair distribution of public goods and services, embedded notions of social hierarchy, and political structures that protect privilege and resist change.

Some of the opposing Yellow Shirt rhetoric was equally premised on the concept of inequality. They claimed the Red Shirts were poor and uneducated, and hence less qualified to participate in democracy than they themselves. They dubbed the protestors as "buffaloes," making the inequality of status on par with the difference between man and beast.

Flexible Oligarchy

A recent ILO study on inequality came to a disarmingly simple conclusion about the relationship between economic and political inequality:

> Instead of triggering redistribution, widening inequality can lead to institutions and policies that perpetuate or accelerate it…. Simply put, inequality in economic resources can lead to inequality in political power, which in turn leads to unequal policies that impede efficient incentives and access to opportunities to invest and innovate (Lee and Gerecke 2015: 52).

In *Oligarchy* (2011), the political scientist Jeffrey Winters showed how, across history and across the world, the rich have grabbed political power in order to use it to protect their wealth. His chapter on the US details how, over the 20th century, the US electoral system shifted from representing people to representing the wealth of corporate and individual donors, and how in parallel the taxation system was changed to allow corporations and billionaires to evade progressive tax.

Oligarchy means rule by the few. Winters narrows this to mean the "rich few," but the term is more useful with its original, broader meaning. In the US today, wealth and power roughly coincide so Winters' redefinition works, but elsewhere the few may wish to consolidate status, privilege, and assets other than monetary wealth.

Oligarchy is especially strong in Thailand because the powerful have never been conclusively undermined or strongly challenged.

In Thailand's modern political history, there has been no decisive break or disjuncture involving mass mobilization. There has been no nationalist movement against colonial rule. The revolution against the absolute monarchy in 1932 enjoyed wide support but required no mass mobilization. The communist insurgency of the 1960s and 1970s was located deep in the forests and hills and never swelled into a mass uprising. Peasant movements and labor agitation have been localized. Equally, there has been no war, crisis, or disaster that has undermined the ruling elites. The monarchy recovered from the overthrow of absolutism in 1932. The military recovered from the political crisis of 1992. The politicians and bankers recovered from the financial crisis of 1997.

The modern Thai political system is best viewed as an oligarchy which has never been radically threatened from below. But this oligarchy has not been static. It has constantly evolved, incorporating new groups and power centers, and building internal bonds through networks, patronage ties, and deals. Under the absolute monarchy, a bureaucratic elite developed from the late 19th century, and became entrenched in the public services. From the 1930s to the 1980s, the military high command dominated politics, and developed a belief in its right to rule. As the urban economy grew in the post-war era of development, new business groups grew powerful through their command of wealth, and demanded access to power through connections and through parliamentary politics. As prosperity spread upcountry, and better communications tied the provincial areas more tightly to the capital, a provincial business elite emerged and demanded a share of power. More recently, the senior judiciary and parts of civil society have also become important.

With the emergence of each new center of power, there has been a period of disruption, conflict, and negotiation of a revised distribution of power. Although noble families and old money figure strongly in this oligarchy, this has never been a closed elite. Indeed its resilience has come partly from its openness and flexibility.

The persistence of economic inequality is a function of the strength of oligarchy. The rule of the few is found not only at the national level but also in the operation of institutions at all levels of society. The few rule and prosper by cultivating and defending privileges and monopolies of various kinds, and by opposing extension of the rule of law which might form the foundations for greater equality. Several chapters of this book present case studies of oligarchy at work in politics, in business, and in finance.

In many of Thailand's key institutions, inequities are built into the structure of their operation for the benefit of the few. In Chapter 4 of this book, Sarinee Achavanuntakul, Nathasit Rakkiattiwong and

Wanicha Direkudomsak present a case study of the stock market as such an institution. They detail the laxity in the rules on insider trading, and on their enforcement. They show the importance of politics in the movement of stock prices, and the importance of the market for politics. They suggest some simple reforms following best international practice.

In recent years, several key institutions have launched quasi-academic bodies whose main function is to serve as nodes of elite networking. In Chapter 5, Nualnoi Treerat and Parkpume Vanichaka list these institutions and describe in detail how they operate. The authors argue that these bodies now play an important part in the invisible structure of oligarchic power. They show how the networks are mobilized to lobby for policy changes on behalf of special interest groups. They suggest these bodies are efficient in integrating new centers of power into the hierarchy, but are problematic because they are not transparent. They suggest ways they should be controlled to limit the risks of abuse.

Since the 1997 Asian financial crisis, two mega-groups in the energy sector have become "national champions" spearheading economic growth. In Chapter 6, Nopanun Wannathepsakul shows how these groups enjoy special advantages from a hybrid public-private status, and from special access to power through bureaucratic networks. These advantages have delivered rapid business growth, but pose risks for good governance, free competition, and protection of the environment. Nopanun argues that the policy support for these business groups should be made more transparent so that society understands these risks and exerts pressure to limit them.

Provincial godfathers—dominant families that relied on rough and ready methods in both business and politics—were a prominent part of national and local politics in the 1980s and 1990s. With greater prosperity, the impact of globalization, and more active civil society, their prominence has faded. In Chapter 7, Chaiyon Praditsil and Chainarong Khrueanuan trace the rise of one godfather family, and show how it is negotiating these changes in order to retain dominance in a new era. They argue that further decentralization and more active civil society are needed to reduce the monopolistic practices of these families.

Thailand's oligarchy is flexible within strict limits. In Chapter 8, Ukrist Pathmanand shows how Thaksin Shinawatra constructed an innovative network of political support—not once but twice. While

Thaksin was initially embraced by the oligarchy, his network became too powerful, and included democratic elements that threatened the principle of oligarchy itself, prompting a long campaign to destroy his network. Although other factors also contributed to Thaksin's fall, including his greed and political clumsiness, his case displays the limits of flexible oligarchy.

Towards a Fairer Society

The international debate on inequality, sketched at the opening of this chapter, is about not only inequality but also the role of the state. In the extreme version of neoliberalism, the state should do the very least necessary to allow free-market capitalism to operate. In truth, no states have gone so far, but there has been a general tendency to reduce the state's role in the neoliberal era. Moreover, opponents have floundered in attempts to find a strong intellectual foundation to oppose neoliberal ideology. Piketty has been such a hit because he seems to offer that foundation. He argues that, left un-attended, the capitalist economy will lead to greater social division, greater conflict and multiple failures. States thus have a duty to prevent this by crafting a social order that its members accept as fair.

Over the past generation, Thailand has developed a society with high inequalities of income and wealth. Over the past decade, Thai politics has been in turmoil with the results of four elections overthrown, two military coups, repeated waves of street demonstrations, and a rising trend of political violence. Although these politics have been complicated by many factors, including personalities, in the background are the tensions of an unequal society. People with rising incomes and aspirations are demanding better access to power, a fairer deal, and more respect, and they have discovered the power of elections to achieve their goal. Others who have been accustomed to the privileges of inequality have mobilized in opposition.

Moving beyond this phase of conflict and mutual distrust will take time. Reducing the high levels of inequality in the society will not quell the immediate conflict but is a prerequisite for achieving a more peaceful and coherent society in the long run. The state can assist by removing structural supports for inequality and creating systems and structures that are more equitable. The task is far from impossible. Many countries offer successful examples. One of the most informative is Japan.

Achieving Equality in the Neoliberal Era: Japan

After World War Two, Japan became an unusually egalitarian society because of changes such as land reform, dismantling the old zaibatsu clans, and the introduction of lifetime employment (Moriguchi and Saez 2006; Minami 2008). But from the 1970s, under pressure from global competition and the neoliberal consensus, this policy regime was undermined, especially lifetime employment. Today a third of the Japanese workforce has been casualized (Jones 2007). As a result, inequality in raw income—meaning one's pay packet before tax or transfers such as social security benefits—rose very steeply. By the late 1990s, this crude income inequality was worse in Japan than in Thailand (see the white bars in Figure 1.7).[6]

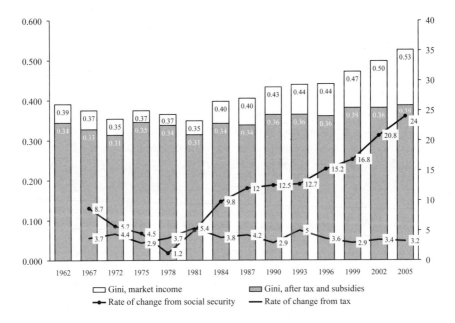

Figure 1.7 Trends in Gini Indices in Japan, 1962–2005

Source: Fujii (2010).

But Japanese governments countered these trends. They made tax more progressive, raising more from the rich than the poor. They increased the amount spent on transfers, particularly pensions, medical benefits, and other subsidies. As a result, household incomes *after tax and transfers* (as shown by the grey bars in Figure 1.7) got worse but only by a small amount. At the start, tax policy contributed most to this equalization, but ultimately transfers contributed by far the most (see the lines in Figure 1.7).

This case has two messages. First, government action can significantly change inequality. Second, pursuing such policies requires political will. Successive Japanese governments pursued this equalizing policy because Japanese people had come to value the benefits of the society's relative egalitarianism.

Japan is not alone in this respect. Luebker (2015: 222–3) shows that many European countries reduce their Gini Index by around 0.2 through tax and transfer policies. Examples include Belgium, Finland, Germany, Poland, Sweden, and the Czech Republic. At the same time, there are some countries with very high inequality which have almost no redistribution mechanisms. There is a sprawling debate in the economic literature on what underlies this difference. Political systems are one factor. Democratic states are more likely to have effective redistribution policies than authoritarian states. But social values seem to be key. Societies which have experienced the benefits of great equality—as in Japan, where hierarchies were levelled after the Second World War, or societies which have had periods of socialism—are more likely to support policies of redistribution. Luebker (2015: 236) concludes that "inequality is not an unavoidable outcome of market forces but—to some degree—a matter of political choice and institutional design."

Public Goods and Budget Constraints

Thailand lacks adequate public goods such as good schools, roads, hospitals, railway trains that stays on the rails, police that do not ask for bribes, publicly minded public prosecutors, and judges that uphold justice. As always, anything in short supply is hoarded by those with power and influence. Public goods are the same.

Public goods and services help people to improve their capabilities to prosper within the market economy and at the same time to make the economy grow. Education is the prime example. If a child from a remote Thai province had the same chance to enter tertiary education as a Bangkok child, then his or her opportunities in life would vastly improve—and her contribution to the economy. As Kobsak (2013) argues, providing good-quality education, and removing economic barriers to access, is the single most important policy the Thai state can pursue to reduce inequality in the long run. Over the past decade, Brazil significantly reduced inequality by increasing the provision of education and providing subsidies for children of the poor (Wetzel 2013). But education is not the only kind of public goods and services that is important in this way. Other public goods work in the same way including good health, social protection against risk, good roads, access to justice, and political and social rights of various kinds.

The principal immediate reason why Thailand lacks public goods and services is the low level of the government budget. Corruption in its use is a secondary cause. From the late 1970s to the present, Thailand's budget has been in the range of 18 to 21 per cent of GDP, well below the average of around 26 per cent for middle-income countries in general (IMF 2010: 25, table 1; World Bank, n.d.).

The budget is small because tax revenues are low. Over 1987–2009, total tax revenue averaged 16.5 per cent of GDP (Pan 2012: 21). TDRI (2015) found that the ratio of tax to GDP was low because many people with high income and considerable assets are able to evade direct taxation. Le, Moreno-Dodson and Jeep (2008: 31) estimated that Thailand could increase tax revenue by 5 per cent of GDP simply by better administration, and even further by removing tax breaks for the wealthy. Somchai Jitsuchon et al. (2011) reckoned that increasing VAT from 7 to 10 per cent would raise a further 2.5 per cent of GDP which would be enough to upgrade current social security systems into a comprehensive social welfare system from child subsidies to old-age pensions, including social security for the large informal workforce.

In Chapter 9 of this book, Pan Ananapibut reviews a range of reforms in the tax system including a revision of income tax exemptions, a negative income tax to aid the poor, and wealth taxes. Several of these suggestions are now under consideration by the Ministry of Finance and the government.

The Politics of Fairness

The policies are not difficult to devise, but is there a political will to enact them? To phrase the question another way: will the oligarchic tendency in Thai politics obstruct any attempts to move towards a fairer society?

The experience of several countries shows that democratic institutions, decentralization and people's movements are the forces that can counter the oligarchic tendency and bring about change. Parliamentary democracy is the only framework that gives people the rights, freedoms, and access to participate in determining policy and pushing for reform. Other systems—including the man on the white horse—promise change but are too easily captured by the oligarchy. The 2014 coup junta announced that it would introduce taxes on wealth as a contribution to reducing inequality. As the first of these, a levy on land and buildings, was about to go to the National Legislative Assembly, the junta withdrew the bill. The generals claimed they feared the impact of this tax on the poor, but the voices raised against the bill had clearly come from the rich. The two major political parties, Democrat and Pheu Thai, also opposed the bill (*Bangkok Post*, Mar. 11 and 13, 2015).

Democratic institutions alone are not enough. At present there is no mechanism for converting mass sentiment into policy. In the theory of parliamentary democracy, political parties should play that role. In Thailand (and many other places in Asia), parties do not work like that. They are not yet structured on democratic lines. In fact they tend to be part of the oligarchic tendency. In recent years, they have been captured by big business groups which invest in politics in expectation of gain from political favors delivering high economic rents (Pramuan and Yupana 2006). Reforms are needed in the administration of government concessions and the policing of fair competition to remove the incentives for big business investing in this way.

More generally, the weak development of Thai political parties is a result of the general immaturity of Thailand's political system. Although there has been an elective parliament for over 80 years, its working has been constantly disrupted by military coups and repeated redrafting of the constitution. The parliament is like an infant who, as soon as she grows up a little and shows some independence, is slapped down and put back in the cradle, and hence never gets a chance to become more mature. And of course, behind these disruptions are forces that wish to preserve inequality, hierarchy and oligarchy.

Achieving change will need the cooperation of many including local leaders and activists, writers, academics, media, NGOs, and political society to support a mentality and culture that supports equity.

Notes

1. The text is at www.whitehouse.gov/the-press-office/2014/01/28/president-barack-obamas-state-union-address [accessed Jan. 1, 2015].
2. The UN and the World Bank prefer the Gini Index of household *expenditure* which is usually lower than that based on income. The Thai literature has always concentrated on the income index which includes the excess of income over expenditure, that is, saving, which contributes to inequality of wealth.
3. The "capability approach" refers to an approach to welfare economics developed by Amartya Sen and others in the 1980s. Economic policy should develop the capability of people to live more productive and fulfilling lives. Good health, higher education, higher income, and political freedoms are some major examples of the capabilities that should be enhanced under this approach.
4. This chart was first drawn by Professor Hal Hill of the Australian National University over a decade ago, and has been updated here with more recent data.
5. Speaking at the Foreign Correspondents Club of Thailand, Apr. 7, 2015.
6. This chart is adapted from a presentation by Yasuhiro Fujii (2010), deputy assistant minister for international policy planning, minister's secretariat, Ministry of Health, Labor and Welfare.

References

Apichart Sathitniramai, Yukti Mukdawijitra and Niti Pawakapan. 2013. *Raingan wijai chabap sombun khrongkan wijai thopthuan phumithat kanmueang thai phaen ngan sangsoem nayobai satharana thi di* [Final Report on the Research Project to Review the Thai Political Landscape, in Support of Good Public Policy]. Bangkok: Thailand Research Fund.

Asia Foundation. 2013. *Profile of the Protestors: A Survey of Pro and Anti-Government Demonstrators in Bangkok on November 30, 2013*. Bangkok: Asia Foundation.

Berg, Andrew, Jonathan D. Ostry and Jeromin Zettelmeyer. 2008. "What Makes Growth Sustained?" IMF Working Paper, Number 08/59, Washington: International Monetary Fund. Available at https://www.imf.org/external/pubs/ft/wp/2008/wp0859.pdf [accessed Mar. 25, 2015].

Berg, Janine, ed. 2015. *Labour Markets, Institutions and Inequality: Building Just Societies in the 21st Century*, ed. Janine Berg. Cheltenham, UK: Edward Elgar in association with the International Labour Office.

Bowornsak Uwanno and Navin Damrigan. 2015. "Constitutional Drafting in Thailand." Photocopy distributed on Apr. 7.

Dilaka Lathapipat. 2013. "The Influence of Family Wealth on Educational Attainments of Youths in Thailand." *Economics of Education Review* 37: 240–57.

Fujii, Yasuhiro. 2010. "Policy Frame for Poverty Alleviation." Available at http://www.mhlw.go.jp/english/policy/affairs/asean/8th.html [accessed Dec. 1, 2011].

Galbraith, James K. 2012. *Inequality and Instability: A Study of the World Economy Just Before the Great Crisis.* Oxford: Oxford University Press.

Glassman, Jim. 2004. *Thailand at the Margins: Internationalization of the State and the Transformation of Labour.* Oxford: Oxford University Press.

Hyun Hwa Son. 2009. "Is Thailand's Fiscal System Pro-Poor?: Looking from Income and Expenditure Components." Available at http://siteresources. worldbank.org/INTDECINEQ/Resources/WRI%28combined%29.pdf [accessed Dec. 1, 2011].

Hewison, Kevin. 2015. "Inequality and Politics in Thailand." *Kyoto Review of Southeast Asia* 17 (March). Available at http://kyotoreview.org/issue-17/inequality-and-politics-in-thailand-2/ [accessed Mar. 25, 2015].

Ikemoto, Y. 1991. *Income Distribution in Thailand: Its Changes, Causes and Structure.* Tokyo: Institute of Developing Economies.

Ikemoto, Y. and M. Uehara. 2000. "Income Inequality and Kuznets' Hypothesis in Thailand." *Asian Economic Journal* 14, 4: 421–43.

International Monetary Fund (IMF). 2010. *Staff Country Report No. 10/344.* Available at https://www.imf.org/external/pubs/cat/longres.aspx?sk= 24394.0 [accessed Mar. 25, 2015].

Jetin, Bruno. 2012. "Distribution of Income, Labour Productivity and Competitiveness: Is the Thai Labour Regime Sustainable?" *Cambridge Journal of Economics* 36, 4 (June): 869–93.

Jones, Randall S. 2007. *Income Inequality, Poverty and Social Spending in Japan.* OECD Economics Department Working Papers No. 556. Available at http://www.oecd-ilibrary.org/economics/income-inequality-poverty-and-social-spending-in-japan_177754708811 [accessed Mar. 25, 2015].

Keyes, Charles F. 2013. *Finding their Voice: Northeastern Villagers and the Thai State.* Chiang Mai: Silkworm Books.

Khan, Mushtaq and Jomo, Kwame Sundaram, eds. 2000. *Rents, Rent-Seeking and Economic Development: Theory and Evidence in Asia.* Cambridge: Cambridge University Press.

Kobsak Pootrakool. 2013. "Khunaphap kan charoen toepto jak miti khong kan krajai raidai panha lae thang ook" [The Quality of Growth from the Perspective of Income Distribution: Problems and Solutions]. Paper presented at the Bank of Thailand annual seminar, Sept. 19.

Kuhonta, Eric. 2011. *The Institutional Imperative: The Politics of Equitable Development in Southeast Asia.* Stanford: Stanford University Press.

Le, Tuan Minh, Blanca Moreno-Dodson and Jeep Rojchaichainthorn. 2008. *Expanding Taxable Capacity and Reaching Revenue Potential: Cross Country Analysis.* Working Paper Series No. 4559, World Bank, March. Available at https://openknowledge.worldbank.org/handle/10986/6565 [accessed Mar. 25, 2015].

Lee, Sangheon and Megan Gerecke. 2015. "Economic Development and Inequality: Revisiting the Kuznets Curve." In *Labour Markets, Institutions and Inequality: Building Just Societies in the 21st Century,* ed. Janine Berg. Cheltenham, UK: Edward Elgar in association with the International Labour Office, pp. 39–64.

Luebker, Malte. 2015. "Redistribution Policies." In *Labour Markets, Institutions and Inequality: Building Just Societies in the 21st Century,* ed. Janine Berg. Cheltenham, UK: Edward Elgar in association with the International Labour Office, pp. 211–41.

Medhi Krongkaew. 1993. "Poverty and Income Distribution." In *The Thai Economy in Transition,* ed. Peter G. Warr. Cambridge: Cambridge University Press, pp. 401–37.

Minami, Ryoshin. 2008. "Income Distribution of Japan: Historical Perspective and Its Implications." *Japan Labour Review* 5, 4: 5–20.

Moriguchi, Chiaki and Emmanuel Saez. 2006. "The Evolution of Income Concentration in Japan 1886–2002: Evidence from Income Tax Statistics." National Bureau of Economic Research Working Paper 12558, October. Available at http://www.nber.org/papers/w12558 [accessed Mar. 25, 2015].

Naruemon Thabchumpon and Duncan McCargo. 2013. "Urbanized Villagers in the 2010 Thai Redshirt Protests: Not Just Poor Farmers?" *Asian Survey* 51, 6: 993–1018.

NESDB (National Economic and Social Development Board). 2014. *Raingan kan wikhro sathanakan khwam yak jon lae khwam loemlam nai prathet that pi 2555* [Report on Poverty and Inequality in Thailand, 2012]. Bangkok: NESDB.

Nualnoi Treerat. 2008. "Khun Charoen and the Liquor Industry through Crisis and Liberalization." In *Thai Capital after the 1997 Crisis,* ed. Pasuk Phongpaichit and Chris Baker. Chiang Mai: Silkworm Books, pp. 129–54.

————. 2013. "The Universal Healthcare Scheme and the Healthcare Market in Thailand." In *Essays on Thailand's Economy and Society. For Professor Chatthip Nartsupha at 72,* ed. Pasuk Phongpaichit and Chris Baker. Bangkok: Sangsan, pp. 275–86.

Obama, Barack. 2014. "President Barack Obama's State of the Union Address." Jan. 28. Available at www.whitehouse.gov/the-press-office/2014/01/28/president-barack-obamas-state-union-address [accessed Jan. 1, 2015].

Organisation for Economic Cooperation and Development (OECD). 2014. *Focus on Inequality and Growth*. Paris: OECD. Available at www.oecd. org/els/soc/Focus-Inequality-and-Growth-2014.pdf [accessed Mar. 25, 2015].

Palma, José Gabriel. 2011. "Homogeneous Middles vs. Heterogeneous Tails, and the End of the 'Inverted-U': The Share of the Rich is What it's all about." Cambridge Working Papers in Economics (CWPE) 1111. Available at http://www.econ.cam.ac.uk/dae/repec/cam/pdf/cwpe1111. pdf [accessed Mar. 25, 2015].

Pan Ananapibut. 2012. "Kan patirup phasi phuea sangkhom thai samoe na" [Tax reform for an equitable Thailand]. Full research report available at http://www.econ.chula.ac.th/research/project?topic=Poli_Topic.

Pasuk Phongpaichit and Pornthep Benyaapikul. 2013. *The Political Economy of a Middle Income Trap: Thailand's Challenges and Opportunities for Reform, A Research Report with support from the Asia Foundation, 2013*. Available at http://www.econ.chula.ac.th/research/book?book=b074.html [accessed Mar. 25, 2015].

Piketty, Thomas. 2014. *Capital in the Twenty-First Century*. Cambridge, Massachusetts, London, England: Belknap Press of Harvard University Press.

Pinkaew Laungaramsri, ed. 2013. *Becoming Red: Kamnoet lae phatthanakan suea daeng nai Chiang Mai* [Birth and Development of Red Shirts in Chiang Mai]. Chiang Mai: Chiang Mai University.

Pramuan Bunkanwanicha and Yupana Wiwattanakantang. 2006. "Big Business Owners and Politics: Investigating the Economic Incentives for Holding Public Office." Center for Economic Institutions Working Paper Series, No. 2006-10. Available at http://hermes-ir.lib.hit-u.ac.jp/ rs/bitstream/10086/13486/1/wp2006-10a.pdf [accessed Apr. 2, 2015].

Rosanvallon, P. 2013. *The Society of Equals*. Translated by Arthur Goldhammer. Cambridge, MA: Harvard University Press.

Somchai Jitsuchon et al. 2011. *Su rabop sawatdikan sangkhom thuan na phai nai phi 2560* [Towards a Comprehensive Social Welfare System by 2017]. Bangkok: Thailand Development Research Institute.

Somchai Phatharathananunth. 2012. "The Politics of Postpeasant Society: The Emergence of the Rural Red Shirts in Northeast Thailand." Unpublished paper.

Sopranzetti, Claudio. 2012. *Red Journeys: Inside the Thai Red Shirt Movement*. Chiang Mai: Silkworm Books.

Stiglitz, J.E. 2011. "Of the 1%, by the 1%, for the 1%." *Vanity Fair*, May. Available at www.vanityfair.com/news/2011/05/top-one-percent-201105 [accessed Mar. 22, 2012].

————. 2012. *The Price of Inequality: How Today's Divided Society Endangers Our Future*. New York: W.W. Norton.

Thailand Development Research Institute (TDRI). 2015. *Kan patirup setthakit phuea lot khwam khatyaeng thang kanmueang* [Economic Reform to Reduce Political Conflict]. Bangkok: TDRI.

United Nations Development Programme (UNDP). 2015. *Advancing Human Development through the ASEAN Community.* Thailand Human Development Report. Bangkok: UNDP.

Walker, Andrew. 2012. *Thailand's Political Peasants: Power in the Modern Rural Economy.* Madison: University of Wisconsin Press.

Warr, Peter. 2003. "Fiscal Policies and Poverty Incidence: The Case of Thailand." *Asian Economic Journal* 17, 1: 27–44.

Wetzel, Deborah. 2013. "Bolsa Família: Brazil's Quiet Revolution." Available at http://www.worldbank.org/en/news/opinion/2013/11/04/bolsa-familia-Brazil-quiet-revolution [accessed Mar. 25, 2015].

Wilkinson, R. and K. Pickett. 2009. *The Spirit Level: Why More Equal Societies Almost Always Do Better.* London: Allen Lane.

Winters, Jeffrey A. 2011. *Oligarchy.* Cambridge: Cambridge University Press.

World Bank. 2009. *Thailand Social Monitor 2009: Towards a Higher Education System in a Global Economy.* Bangkok: World Bank.

———. 2012. *Improving Service Delivery. Thailand: Public Finance Management Report.* Bangkok: World Bank.

———. n.d. "Expense (% of GDP)." Available at http://data.worldbank.org/indicator/GC.XPN.TOTL.GD.ZS [accessed Mar. 25, 2015].

2

Concentration of Land and Other Wealth in Thailand

Duangmanee Laovakul

Until recently, studies of economic inequality in Thailand have focused on income rather than wealth, in part because data for analyzing wealth were not available. There have been several attempts to analyze the distribution of landholding, but these were based on partial data as no national database was available. Recently, this situation has changed in two ways. First, in 2006, the regular Socio-Economic Survey that generates the data for analyzing income distribution also collected data on household ownership of assets for the first time. The same data were also collected in 2007 and 2009. Second, the Land Department has computerized its database on titled landholding, and gave access to this team to analyze this data for the first time.[1] Hence, this chapter presents the first-ever analysis of the distribution of land on a national scale based on the record of land titles, along with a summary of the Socio-Economic Survey's findings on the distribution of wealth, and a review of other information on wealth inequality.

The analysis of these new data on the distribution of land and other assets shows that wealth is extremely concentrated in Thailand, even more so than income. This finding has important implications for taxation policy.

The Distribution of Land

The surface area of Thailand in total is around 320 million rai (51.2 million hectare).[2] Subtracting areas of forests and parks, public land,

and plots under temporary or special titles leaves 95 million rai (14.4 million hectare) under the regular land title, known as *chanot*, which confers full legal rights to sell, transfer or mortgage the land. Henceforth this will be called "titled land."

In 2012, there were around 15.9 million owners of titled land (Table 2.1). Of these, 98.7 per cent were individuals and the others were juristic persons, meaning corporations, foundations, associations or other juristic bodies of some kind.

The Gini Index for the distribution of all titled land nationwide in 2012 was 0.886. For individuals the figure was 0.881 and for juristic persons 0.953.

Table 2.1 Holdings of Titled Land Nationwide, 2012

Owners	Total Landholding		Average Holding		Gini Index
	rai	%	rai	ha	
Total	15,900,047	100.0	5.968	0.955	0.886
Individuals	15,687,551	98.7	5.690	0.910	0.881
Juristic persons	212,496	1.3	26.462	4.234	0.953

Source: Author's calculations from Land Department data.

Concentration of land ownership is highest in Bangkok and the Central region (Gini Index of 0.92) and lowest in the Northeast (0.86) but the regional difference is not very wide (Table 2.2).

Table 2.2 Distribution of Titled Land by Region, 2012

Region	Number of Landowners	Gini Index
Nationwide	15,900,047	0.89
Bangkok	1,526,297	0.92
Center	4,626,094	0.92
North	3,138,428	0.88
Northeast	5,257,734	0.85
South	1,838,529	0.86

Source: Author's calculations from Land Department data.

The top 10 per cent of all holders (individuals and juristic persons combined) hold over three-fifths of all land, and the bottom 10 per cent own just 0.07 per cent (Figure 2.1). The ratio between the total land held by the top fifth and the bottom fifth is 326 times. The gradient at the top end of the land distribution is especially steep; see the difference between the last two bars in Figure 2.1.

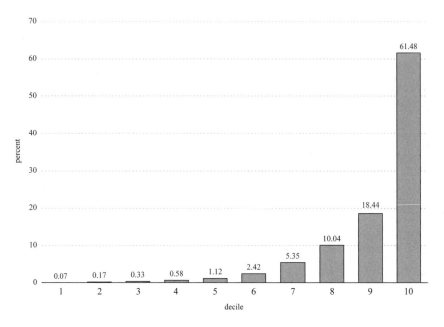

Figure 2.1　Distribution of Titled Land by Decile, 2012
Source: Author's calculations from Land Department data.

Around one half of all landholders (50.17 per cent) own less than one rai, and another fifth (21.9 per cent) own between 1 and 5 rai (Table 2.3).

Across the country there were 837 owners with over 1,000 rai (160 ha) including 359 individuals and 487 juristic persons. The largest holding, held by an individual, was 631,263 rai (101,002 ha).

The Gini Index of 0.886 for the nationwide land distribution compares to a Gini of 0.485 for household income. These figures indicate that the concentration of land ownership in Thailand is very high. Over a third of the population still makes its primary living in agriculture, where land is a vital resource. The 2010 census found that around 4.5 million households do not own a house. As in many countries, land is a favored form of savings and investment. Yet a tenth of holders control three-fifths of total land, and over 70 per cent of all holdings are less than 5 rai.

Table 2.3 Number of Landowners Classified by Size of Holding, 2012

Size of Land	Number of Landowners	Per cent
1–10 sq.wa	285,952	1.80
10–20 sq.wa	884,467	5.56
20–50 sq.wa	1,715,991	10.79
50–100 sq.wa	1,886,025	11.86
100–200 sq.wa	1,760,310	11.07
200–300 sq.wa	844,568	5.31
300 sq.wa to 1 rai	601,815	3.78
1–5 rai	3,482,206	21.90
5–10 rai	1,894,524	11.92
10–15 rai	967,268	6.08
15–20 rai	528,405	3.32
20–25 rai	331,584	2.09
25–30 rai	208,781	1.31
30–35 rai	137,113	0.86
35–40 rai	92,943	0.58
40–45 rai	66,075	0.42
45–50 rai	50,016	0.31
50–100 rai	127,149	0.80
100–500 rai	32,457	0.20
500–1000 rai	1,561	0.01
Over 1000 rai	837	0.01
Total	15,900,047	100.00

Notes: 1 rai = 0.16 hectare, 1 sq.wa. = 4 square meters
Source: Author's calculations from Land Department data.

Landholding by Politicians

In light of these figures, the holdings of land by politicians are of some interest since they have influence over policy affecting land, including taxation. Every MP has to report assets, including land, to the National Counter Corruption Commission, and these data are made public.

In 2013, 507 MPs reported owning some land. The total extent of the land was 35,792 rai (5,727 ha) and its total value was 15.7 billion baht. The single largest holder owned land worth 2.7 billion baht. The average holding was 71.6 rai (11.5 ha), which would fall in the top quintile of all landholders. MPs held land on average worth 30.91 million baht (Table 2.4).

Table 2.4 Land Holding by MPs, June 2013

Party	Number of MPs	Total Landholding		Average Landholding		Value (million baht)	
		rai	ha	rai	ha	Total	Average
Democrat	151	12,675.73	2,028.1	84.95	13.6	6,513.50	43.14
Pheu Thai	282	17,897.27	2,863.6	63.27	10.1	7,131.70	25.29
Phumjai Thai	33	3,034.82	485.6	92.97	14.9	570.54	17.29
Chat Thai Pattana	18	938.61	150.2	52.15	8.3	634.38	35.24
Other	23	1,245.77	199.3	54.16	8.67	819.0	35.60
Total	507	35,792.00	5,726.7	71.60	11.5	15,669.14	30.91

Notes: Some MPs declared just the value, not the size of their land
Source: Calculated from MP asset declarations files, National Counter Corruption Commission.

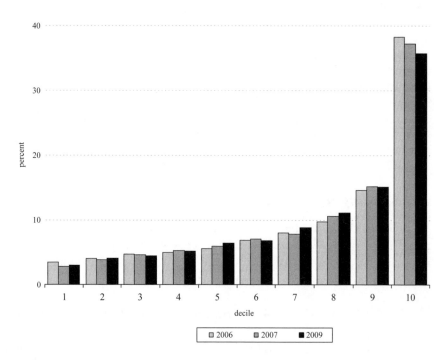

Figure 2.2 Household Asset Distribution by Decile, 2006, 2007 and 2009

Source: Author's calculations from NSO, *Household Socio-Economic Survey*, 2006, 2007 and 2009.

Concentration of Asset Holding by Households

In its Socio-Economic Survey for 2006, 2007 and 2009, the National Statistical Office collected data on household ownership of assets in four categories: land and buildings used for residence; land and buildings used for business, agriculture or other purposes; vehicles; and financial assets. The survey did not cover other categories of wealth such as jewelry, works of art, or other valuables.

The distribution of the total assets covered by these surveys was very unequal. In 2009, the top decile owned 37 per cent of total assets while the bottom decile owned less than 3 per cent. The gradient at the top end of the scale is again very steep, though not as steep as in the case of titled land (Figure 2.2).

The Gini Index of total assets in 2009 was high at 0.656. The Gini for financial assets was notably high at 0.849 (Table 2.5). The variation between the three surveys was slight.

Table 2.5   Gini Index of Asset Distribution in Thailand, 2006, 2007 and 2009

Types of Assets	Gini Index		
	2006	2007	2009
All assets	0.678	0.672	0.656
Houses, land and buildings for residential purpose	0.718	0.703	0.679
Houses, land and buildings for business, agricultural and other purposes	0.882	0.882	0.884
Vehicles	0.757	0.745	0.735
Financial assets	0.852	0.855	0.849

Source: Author's calculations from NSO, *Household Socio-Economic Survey*, 2006, 2007 and 2009.

Concentration of Financial Wealth and Shareholding

Money deposited in banks is also highly concentrated. In December 2013, there were 111,517 bank deposits (current account, savings account or time deposit) with a value over 10 million baht apiece. These 111,517 deposits represented only 0.13 per cent of the total number of bank deposits, but contained 49.24 per cent of the total amount deposited.[3]

Table 2.6 Top 10 Stock Holders on the Stock Exchange of Thailand, 2009–11

	2009		2010		2011	
	Name	Value (bn baht)	Name	Value (bn baht)	Name	Value (bn baht)
1	Anant Asavabhokhin	16.0	Thongma Vijitpongpun	31.4	Thongma Vijitpongpun	18.5
2	Thongma Vijitpongpun	15.8	Keeree Karnjanapas	17.8	Anant Asavabhokhin	15.5
3	Niti Osathanugrah	5.7	Anant Asavabhokhin	17.6	Keeree Karnjanapas	12.7
4	Prawit Maleenont	5.2	Prawit Maleenont	8.9	Wichai Thongtang	11.8
5	Viroj Thanalongkorn	4.4	Worawit Weeraborwornpong	8.8	Prasert Prasarttong-osoth	9.9
6	Worawit Weeraborwornpong	4.3	Niti Osathanugrah	7.7	Sathit Wittayakorn	9.5
7	Paiboon Damrongchaitham	4.3	Viroj Thanalongkorn	6.3	Niti Osathanugrah	7.6
8	Prasert Prasarttong-osoth	4.2	Prachum Maleenont	6.1	Viroj Thanalongkorn	6.3
9	Anuphong Asavabhokhin	3.7	Rattana Maleenont	6.1	Worawit Weeraborwornpong	5.7
10	Prachum Maleenont	3.6	Uamporn Maleenont	6.1	Prateep Tangmatitham	5.4
Total		67.2		117.0		102.9

Source: Money and Banking in cooperation with staff of Chulalongkorn Business School.

For several years, the magazine *Money and Banking* (*Kan ngoen kan thanakan*) has published an annual list of the top shareholders on the Stock Exchange of Thailand. The people on the list vary from year to year, but not by much. Over the three years from 2009 to 2011, five names appeared in all three years, and four others appeared in two (Table 2.6). The magazine also tracks the top holdings by family. In 2011, the top place was taken by the Maleenont family with total shares of 37.9 billion baht, followed by the Vijitpongpun, Chirathiwat, Asavabhokhin, Thongtang, Karnjanapas, Prasarttong-osoth, Chansiri, Mahakitsiri and Sophonpanich families.

Each year *Forbes* magazine publishes a list of Thailand's richest individuals or families with estimates of their net worth. Table 2.7

Table 2.7 Top 20 Richest Families from *Forbes* Magazine, 2008–14

	2014		2011		2008	
	US$ bn	rank	US$ bn	rank	US$ bn	rank
Chirathiwat family	12.70	1	4.30	4	2.80	3
Dhanin Chearavanont & family	11.50	2	7.40	1	2.00	4
Charoen Sirivadhanabhakdi	11.30	3	4.80	3	3.90	2
Chalerm Yoovidhya	9.90	4	5.23	2	4.19	1
Krit Ratanarak	5.10	5	2.50	5	1.00	5
Vanich Chaiyawan	3.90	6	0.93	12	0.39	17
Santi Bhirombhakdi & family	2.80	7	2.00	7	0.82	8
Prasert Prasarttong-osoth	2.30	8	0.62	17	0.25	22
Vichai Maleenont & family	1.70	9	1.50	8	0.88	7
Thaksin Shinawatra & family	1.70	10	0.60	19	0.40	16
Vichai Srivaddhanaprabha	1.60	11	0.21	38	0.19	26
Chatri Sophonpanich	1.60	12				
Rit Thirakomen & family	1.50	13				
Thongma Vijitpongpun	1.40	14	1.00	11	0.38	18
Prayudh Mahakitsiri & family	1.40	15	0.90	13	0.52	12
Keeree Karnjanapas	1.40	16	0.63	16	0.00	0
Boonchai Bencharongkul & family	1.30	17	0.55	20	0.48	13
Aloke Lohia	1.20	18	2.10	6		
Wichai Thongtang	1.10	19				
Isara Vongkusolkit & family	1.10	20	1.40	9	0.47	14

Sources: http://www.forbes.com/thailand-billionaires/list/2/#tab:overall; http://www.forbes.com/lists/2011/85/thailand-billionaires-11_rank.html; http://www.forbes.com/lists/2008/85/biz_thairichest08_Thailands-Richest_Networth.html

shows the 20 top-ranked in the 2014 list, and their positions from the earlier lists in 2011 and 2008. The top five names have been the same in all three years, although the rankings have shifted. The gradient of the relative wealth of these billionaires is rather steep. The top ranked has ten times the wealth of the twentieth. Most strikingly, the wealth of these richest families has increased rapidly in recent years according to *Forbes'* estimates. For three of those in the top five, their estimated wealth has increased around five times in the six years since 2008.

Although a few names have dropped out of these lists over the years, overall the *Forbes'* estimates give a picture of rapid increase at the top end of the wealth scale. The total wealth of the 40 richest families was US$25 billion in 2008, US$45 billion in 2011, and US$93 billion in 2014—roughly doubling every three years (while inflation averaged around 2 per cent per year). Of the top 40 on the *Forbes* list in 2014, 28 appeared on the 2011 list and their total estimated wealth had doubled between 2011 and 2014, while 26 appeared on the 2008 list and their wealth had multiplied 3.4 times between 2008 and 2014. These rates of increase far outstrip inflation or GDP growth.

Conclusion

Wealth is very highly concentrated in Thailand. The first analysis of land distribution based on nationwide land title data shows that 10 per cent of all landholders, roughly 1.5 million individuals or organizations, own over three-fifths of total land. The first surveys of household ownership of assets show a Gini Index for asset distribution of around 0.66. Estimates by *Forbes* magazine shows that accumulations of wealth are increasing rapidly at the top end of the scale, roughly doubling every three years.

As discussed in Chapter 1, one reason for inequality in Thailand is the under-supply of public goods and services. There are too few good schools, inadequate public transport facilities, and no comprehensive provision for old age even though the society is rapidly ageing.

Increasing the supply of public goods and services can have a significant impact on poverty and inequality. This has been demonstrated in Thailand by the Universal Health Care scheme launched over a decade ago (Nualnoi 2013). An assessment of the first ten years (2001–10) of the scheme showed that household expenditures on healthcare had decreased, especially in poor households, and that the number of households that dropped below the poverty line because of health expenditure had significantly fallen (Health Insurance Systems Research Office 2012).[4]

One major reason for the under-supply of public goods and services is the limitation of the government budget. As also discussed in Chapter 1, Thailand has a rather low rate of taxation to GDP. Any scheme to increase public revenue should be based on the principle of "ability to pay." Given the very high concentration of wealth in Thailand, taxation on assets will fall on relatively few people who have very high ability to pay. For this reason, a land tax, wealth tax, or tax on capital gains that yields revenue which can be spent on increasing the supply of public goods will have a positive impact on inequality.

Notes

1. The ownership data were anonymous, with owners identified by codes.
2. This sum total can be divided as follows (figures in million rai): Forestry Department (reserved forests and parks, 2011 data), 144.54; Agricultural Reform Office (resettlement schemes, 2013 data), 34.76; Treasury Department (public land, 2012 data), 9.78; Land Department (2012 data), 130.74. These figures sum to 319.82, slightly less than the true total of 320.70, because the data come from various years. Of the 130.74 million rai under the Land Department, 95 million rai are covered by *chanot* titles, and the remainder by various forms of temporary title (SK1, NS3, NS3k, etc.), which mostly allow occupancy but are not technically transferable. These data await future analysis.
3. Calculated from Bank of Thailand table Fl_CB_018_S2, accessible through http://www.bot.or.th/Thai/Statistics/FinancialInstitutions/ CommercialBank/Pages/index.aspx
4. The assessment estimated that the number of households falling below the poverty line due to health expenditure had fallen from 2.7 per cent in 2000 to 0.49 per cent in 2009. A total of 219,790 households were prevented from falling into poverty over the period 2004–09.

References

Department of Lands, Ministry of Interior. Land data.

Health Insurance System Research Office. 2012. *Thailand's Universal Coverage Scheme: Achievements and Challenges, An Independent Assessment of the First 10 Years (2001–2010)*. Nonthaburi: Health Insurance System Research Office.

Money and Banking magazine (*Kan ngoen kan thanakan*). 2009–11.

National Statistical Office (NSO). *Household Socio-Economic Survey*, 2006, 2007 and 2009.

Nualnoi Treerat. 2013. "The Universal Healthcare Scheme and the Healthcare Market in Thailand." In *Essays on Thailand's Economy and Society: For Professor Chatthip Nartsupha at 72*, ed. Pasuk Phongpaichit and Chris Baker. Bangkok: Sangsan, pp. 275–86.

3

Inequality in Education and Wages

DILAKA LATHAPIPAT

Education is important both for the individual and society. A higher level and better quality of education helps improve the labor market opportunities, economic position, and social status of the individual, and efficient management of education can help to reduce income disparity and social inequality.

The average level of education in Thailand has increased steadily in line with economic development, but with a high level of variation, both in the quality of basic education, and the opportunity to enter tertiary education. This inequality arises from the difference in the economic and social status of households.

When a youth from a disadvantaged household does not have the opportunity to gain a higher level and quality of education, both the individual and Thailand as a society sacrifice the potential benefit.

This chapter presents data on inequality in education and the factors behind it. The analysis is divided into three parts. The first presents an overview of changes in the access to education, with analysis of the short and long term factors which affect enrolment at the upper secondary and tertiary levels. The second part examines the relationship between education level and labor market price, along with trends of change in the gap between groups with different levels of education. The third analyzes the variation in wages among those with the same level of education.

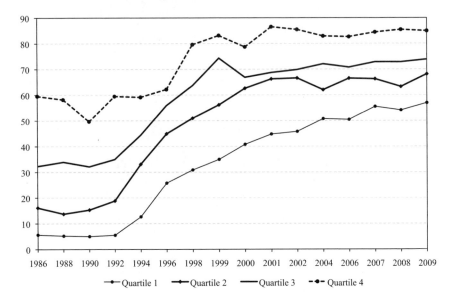

Figure 3.1 Change in Upper Secondary Enrolment by Household Income Quartile, 1986–2009

Source: National Statistical Office, *Household Socio-Economic Survey*, various years.

An Overview of Inequality in Education

Thailand has been rather successful in expanding access to education. The average years of schooling of those in the labor force (aged 16–65 years) increased from 5.3 in 1986 to 8.3 in 2010. Over this period, the proportion of the labor force with less than 6 years of primary education fell steeply from 68 to 29 per cent, while the proportion of those with tertiary below BA degree level grew from 2.2 to 5.3 per cent, and those of BA level from 2.7 to 12.2 per cent.

This rapid increase went hand-in-hand with growing disparity between socioeconomic groups. Although inequality in access to education has declined at the upper secondary level, it has increased at the tertiary level.

The enrolment rate beyond the compulsory three years of secondary schooling into the upper secondary level (aged 16–19 years) has increased rapidly, and the variation between socioeconomic groups has narrowed (Figure 3.1). The proportion of children from the lowest income quartile (the bottom 25 per cent of households measured by per-capita consumption spending) has increased from

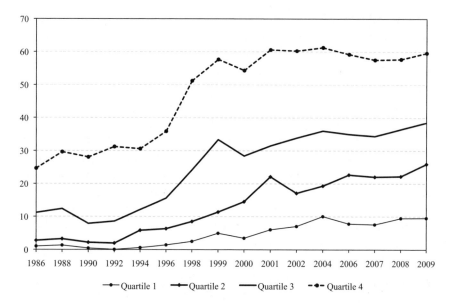

Figure 3.2 Change in College Enrolment by Household Income Quartile, 1986–2009

Source: National Statistical Office, *Household Socio-Economic Survey*, various years.

5.6 to 57.0 per cent over the period 1986 to 2010, and the gap between the top and bottom quartiles has narrowed from 54 to 28 percentage points.

By contrast, inequality in access to college level has increased steeply (Figure 3.2). The gap in the enrolment rate between the richest and poorest quartiles increased from 24 to 50 percentage points between 1986 and 2009. Significantly, the gap widened markedly after 1996, the year of establishing an Education Loan Fund intended to overcome the financial constraint on access to tertiary education. It appears that children of poor households got fewer benefits from this fund than those of better economic status.

Such a widening gap in the participation of college education between the rich and the poor hinders social mobility and further widens income inequality across the generations.

Factors Determining Access to Education[1]

The factors which explain the highest education level attained can be divided into long and short term. The long-term factors include the educational level of parents, place of abode, socio-economic status of the household, number of household members, and variables that indicate family warmth (such as whether the whole family lives together). The main short-term factor is the household's income or economic status at the time when the decision is taken whether a child will continue to the next stage of education.

Which of these factors is important in determining access to education has implications for policy-making to reduce inequality. If the variation in enrolment is a result of the household's economic status, policy should try to reduce the financial burden on disadvantaged households. But if the variation arises from long-term factors, policies that reduce the financial burden will not help to reduce the inequality. Instead, more long-term policies will be needed to address the biases arising from these long-term factors.

Household Income is of Growing Importance

I investigated the relative importance of household income and other long-run family factors in determining educational attainment (that is, the highest level of education attained), and found three main points. First, the household's economic status is the key factor determining educational attainment for all groups and all ages. Second, the gap between rural and urban youth was wide at the beginning, but diminished steadily from 1991 onwards—a result of the policy of increasing access to education in the provincial regions.

Third, children who enroll at tertiary level come from households with a higher average income than those of children who have a lower educational attainment. For example, the monthly average real household income of male college students and high school graduates in the 1991 cohort were 30,800 and 17,500 respectively, a difference of 1.8 times. This ratio dropped to 1.5 times by 1997 but increased again to 1.6 times in 2008. For females, the pattern was the same.

A Key Difference Between the Upper Secondary and Tertiary Levels

As a result of government policy to provide universal access to basic education up to high school completion without charge,[2] household characteristics have had a steadily diminishing role in determining access to the upper secondary level. In addition, as a result of an implicit no-fail policy in Thai schools, the importance of educational capability has also diminished at this level. Hence, at a time when upper secondary enrolment was increasing for all socioeconomic groups, those who dropped out must have done so because of the high indirect costs of education, or the need or desire to earn income in the labor market.

At the tertiary level, both household characteristics and household income have contributed to the increased disparity across all socio-economic groups. Household characteristics have more influence on enrolment rates at the tertiary level, compared to the upper secondary level, though their influence is again on a declining trend, while the short-term factor of household income is of increasing importance for youth in the lower socioeconomic groups.

How Many Children are Missing Out and Why

I estimated how many youth who complete their education at the upper secondary level could not continue to the tertiary level because of financial constraints,[3] and found that the proportion increased from 14.3 per cent in 1991 to 19.3 per cent in 2008. When I then removed the influence of the long-term household characteristics from the estimation, the figures fell to 5.1 and 11.4 per cent respectively. This estimation confirms that household income plays an increasing role in limiting continuation to the tertiary level.

The surge in the relative importance of family income could have resulted from the rapidly increasing cost of college education. It could also have come about because relatively rich but less able youths account for a larger share of the recent increase in college enrolment.[4]

Declining Scholastic Ability

What then is the relationship between family background and the quality of a child's educational attainment? To investigate this point, I examined the relationship between socioeconomic background and scores for science and mathematics in the 2006 Programme for International Student Assessment (PISA)[5] for 15-year-old students.

PISA has an Economic, Social and Cultural Status (ESCS) index for each student. The index is computed from data on the occupation, educational status, financial status and cultural factors of the parents of the students. Calculating from the sample of 210 schools in the 2006 PISA results, the average ESCS index of a school explains 67 per cent of the variation of the average PISA score attained by each school.

In addition, between 2000 and 2009, the PISA scores of Thai students at all levels and in all disciplines declined by a small amount. This means that the output from tertiary education has increased at a time that the average scholastic ability of the student input has been declining.

Wage Inequality among Educational Groups

The growing inequality at the top of the educational system is reflected and magnified by changes in the labor market.

To study the dispersion of wages, those in the labor force were classified into six groups according to the highest level of education attained: some-primary; completed-primary; some-secondary; completed-secondary; some-tertiary; and completed-tertiary. For simplicity, only four are shown in the charts, omitting the some-primary and some-secondary groups. Figure 3.3 shows that, in the period

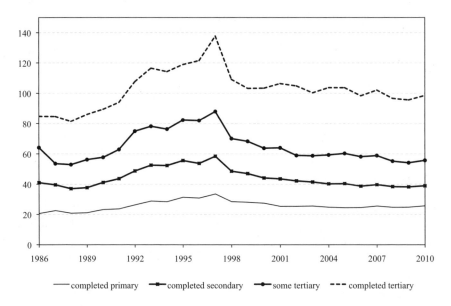

Figure 3.3 Real Hourly Wage Rates by Education Group, 1986–2010

Note: unit is baht at 2009 prices
Source: National Statistical Office, *Labour Force Survey*, various years.

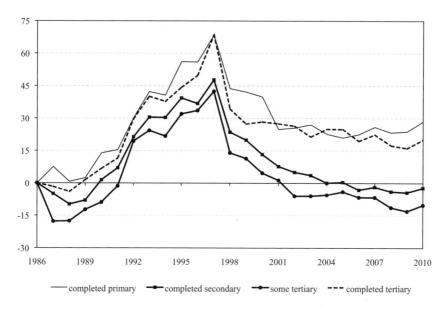

—— completed primary —■— completed secondary —●— some tertiary --- completed tertiary

Figure 3.4 Rate of Change of Hourly Wage Rates by Education Group, 1986–2010

Note: unit is index where 1986 = 0
Source: National Statistical Office, *Labour Force Survey*, various years.

when the Thai economy was growing rapidly, the wage rate increased for all education groups, while after the crisis of 1997, wages of all groups fell steeply, and remained depressed until 2010.

To see variation between education groups, the wage rates were converted into indices based on the year 1986. Figure 3.4 shows clearly that wage rates became more polarized from 1986 until the financial crisis of 1997. The average real wage of the completed-primary group and the completed-tertiary group increased by 68.4 and 68.6 per cent respectively while those of the completed-secondary and some-tertiary groups increased by only 47.7 and 42.4 per cent respectively. After the financial crisis the average wage of all groups tended to decline, but at greatly different rates. The steepest declines were for the completed-secondary and some-tertiary groups. By 2010, the average real wage of these two groups had fallen below their level in 1986. The polarization of wages between different education groups has been marked.

To analyze inequality in the upper part of the wage structure, I divided the labor force into two groups based on education: those with tertiary-equivalent and those with upper secondary-equivalent. As can be inferred from Figures 3.3 and 3.4 above, the gap between the average wage rates of these two groups has widened over time. Most interestingly, the widening of the wage gap has occurred despite a simultaneous increase in the relative supply of tertiary-equivalent labor. This can only occur if the demand for labor with a tertiary degree has increased faster than the demand for labor with a secondary qualification.[6]

Possibly this variation in the trend of demand was a result of changes in production technology which increased the efficiency of those with a higher level of education more than that of those with a lower level (skill-biased technological change). Alternatively it may have been a result of increased demand for products that require high-skilled labor in production, or changes in the prices of other factors of production that can be substituted for labor or that have different impact on the productivity of different groups (Autor, Katz and Krueger 1998).

Inequality of Wages within Groups of Same Skill

The analysis so far has focused on differences between groups with different educational levels. But there may also have been change in the wage dispersion within each educational group. Such dispersion is very important from the angle of policy making. A study by Juhn, Murphy and Pierce (1993) found that some wage inequality was a result of factors other than education level and working experience, including factors such as inequality of capability, quality of education received, commitment, and capacity for hard work that cannot be detected from the usual labor market data.[7]

In the Thai case, wage inequality has increased, even within the completed-tertiary group. Between 1986 and 2010, the real wage rate of the top 10 per cent of those with completed-tertiary education increased by around 45 per cent, while the average real wage of the bottom 10 per cent of those with completed-tertiary education fell by 15 per cent (Figure 3.5).

This increased variation may stem from the rapid expansion in the number of places in tertiary education in recent years, admitting more and more students with less than high ability, resulting in greater variation in the *quality* of education among those graduating at tertiary level. This conclusion agrees with the evidence from the

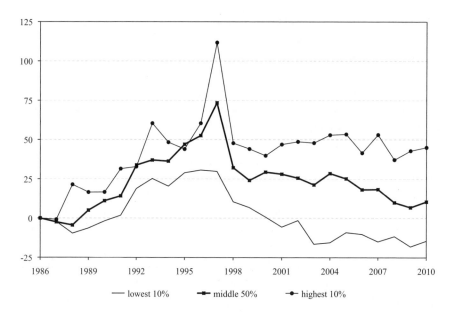

Figure 3.5 Rate of Change of Hourly Wage within Completed-Tertiary Group, 1986–2010

Note: unit is index where 1986 = 0
Source: National Statistical Office, *Labour Force Survey*, various years.

falling trend of PISA scores for Thai students. My hypothesis is that youth in later cohorts who continue to the tertiary level on average have lower average scholastic ability than earlier cohorts.

Conclusion

In the recent past, Thailand has been rather successful in expanding access to basic education. As a result, the inequality in access to upper secondary education among different socioeconomic groups has diminished. However, inequality in many aspects of education is still marked.

Youth from socially and economically disadvantaged households have fewer opportunities to enter tertiary education than youth from more privileged households. These children are not only disadvantaged in education, but also in the wages they will receive when entering the labor market in the future. In addition, the financial status of the household has become increasingly important in determining which students continue to the tertiary level. I suspect that increasing numbers of those who continue to the tertiary level are students who come from households of good financial status but who on average have lower scholastic ability than earlier cohorts. This is a result of the rapid expansion of places in tertiary institutions, combined with the increasing importance of income in gaining access, and the decline in the quality of Thai school students, as shown by the downward trend in PISA scores.

Although the short-term factor of household income is increasingly important for determining continuation to the tertiary level, long-run household characteristics (parents' education, location, etc.) still retain some importance. This means that the existing high inequality in access to the tertiary level cannot be eradicated by increasing educational loans or subsidies alone. There must also be long-term policies to raise the level of scholastic ability of youth that come from socially and economically disadvantaged households, beginning with proper preparation in the pre-school phase, and better basic education in schools which service children from disadvantaged households.

The wage gap between those completing tertiary and those completing upper secondary has increased steadily over the study period. This has come about even though the supply of tertiary graduates in the labor force has increased faster than the supply of secondary school graduates. This suggests that the demand for BA graduates has increased more than the demand for those completing upper secondary. Partly this may be a result of changes in the technology of production and service sectors which favor labor with higher skill levels.

Finally, there is increased variation in the wages of those with completed tertiary education. Most likely this is a result of increasing variability in the *quality* of graduates at the tertiary level. I suspect that this may be a result of tertiary institutions, private and public, offering many new courses in order to meet the increasing student demand for degrees, without paying sufficient attention to quality or market demand. The result is the production of low quality graduates, often from faculties that do not match with market demand.

Providing fair access to good-quality education that meets the needs of the labor market is one of the best ways to reduce social inequality in the long run. Thailand's reforms in extending compulsory secondary education and increasing subsidies have been largely effective at the secondary level, but less so at the tertiary level. This study identifies two areas for reform. First, fair access to good-quality schooling from the earliest stage onwards is needed to eliminate the variation in performance that accumulates through the education system and results in starkly different levels of access to the tertiary level. Second, the courses offered by institutions at the tertiary level need to be better aligned with the demands of the labor market.

Notes

1. To analyze the education level of the Thai labor force, we should consider what factors affected the decisions of members of the labor force to study to what level of education, including factors related to the economic and social condition of the household, and indicators of scholastic ability. However, data for variables indicating scholastic ability are not available, and most labor market data come from cross-section studies, so we lack crucial information on their family income and living environment at the time decisions were made on their schooling. In addition, many of those in the labor force did not reside with their parents during their education. To circumvent these problems, I focus the study on youths aged 16–24 years who are living with their parent(s), for whom we have social and economic data on the household at or close to the time of education. The type of economic model suitable for data with this limitation is the censored ordered probit/logit model developed by King and Lillard (1983, 1987).

    For a detailed account of the calculations summarized here, see Lathapipat (2013).

2. The 1997 Constitution was the first to state in Article 43 that "A person shall enjoy an equal right to receive the fundamental education for the duration of not less than twelve years which shall be provided by the State thoroughly, up to the quality, and without charge."

3. For this estimation I used the method of Carneiro and Heckman (2002).

4. However, without a direct measure of cognitive ability, this is at best a speculation. In addition readers should be aware that this study cannot control completely for long-term factors.

5. PISA is an OECD standard for measuring 15-year-old students' competency in the key areas of reading, mathematics, and science; see www.nces.ed.gov/surveys/pisa/.

6. A model was constructed to study the roles of supply and demand in the comparative trends of wages for secondary-equivalent and tertiary-equivalent labor groups. It follows that, if the structure of comparative demand for tertiary-equivalent workers does not change but the comparative supply increases, the wage gap between the tertiary-equivalent

and secondary-equivalent groups will narrow. However, if the wage gap widens then the comparative demand for tertiary-equivalent workers must be increasing faster than the comparative supply. Thus, the change in the structure of demand is chiefly responsible for increasing disparity of wages, especially in the upper part of the wage structure.

7. To account for the variation of these unobserved factors, I begin by estimating a wage equation in the style of Mincer, by using the econometric method known as unconditional quantile regression developed by Firpo, Fortin and Lemieux (2006, 2009). This method enables me to estimate the trend of change in hourly wages for various percentiles within each labor force group, while controlling the major characteristics of labor, such as work experience and domicile, to remain constant throughout the study.

References

Autor, D.H., L.F. Katz and A.B. Krueger. 1998. "Computing Inequality: Have Computers Changed the Labor Market?" *Quarterly Journal of Economics* 113, 4 (Nov.): 1169–214.

Carneiro, P. and J.J. Heckman. 2002. "The Evidence on Credit Constraints in Post-Secondary Schooling." *Economic Journal* 112: 989–1018.

Firpo, S., N.M. Fortin and T. Lemieux. 2006. "Unconditional Quantile Regressions." PUC Rio: Working Paper 533.

————. "Unconditional Quantile Regressions." *Econometrica* 77, 3: 953–73.

Juhn, C., K.M. Murphy and B. Pierce. 1993. "Wage Inequality and the Rise in Returns to Skill." *Journal of Political Economy* 101, 3: 410–42.

King, E. and L. Lillard. 1983. "Determinants of Schooling Attainment and Enrollment Rates in the Philippines." *Rand Report # N-1962-AID*.

————. 1987. "Education Policy and Schooling Attainment in Malaysia and the Philippines." *Economics of Education Review* 6, 2: 167–81.

Lathapipat, Dilaka 2013. "The Influence of Family Wealth on the Educational Attainments of Youths in Thailand." *Economics of Education Review* 37: 240–57.

4

Inequality, the Capital Market and Political Stocks

SARINEE ACHAVANUNTAKUL, NATHASIT RAKKIATTIWONG
AND WANICHA DIREKUDOMSAK

Economic inequality reflects injustice in the social structure. It tends to reduce the rate of economic growth (Barro 1999), obstruct the inclusive economy necessary for sustainable development, and foster social conflict and distrust among people of differing statuses. In *The Spirit Level*, Richard Wilkinson and Kate Pickett (2009) argued that reducing inequality is not only an ethical issue, but a strategy for bringing benefits to people of all walks of life since inequality is the root cause of many social problems such as crimes, obesity, unwanted pregnancies among youth, and depression.

All the institutions which form the structural context of the economy have implications for inequality. One of the key institutions is the capital market, and in particular the stock exchange. This chapter examines how the operation of the capital market affects inequality both inside and outside the market. The chapter has four sections. The first reviews the inequality in wealth and asset holding in Thailand within an international context. The second examines the linkages between the capital market and some aspects of economic inequality. The third presents a case study of abnormal returns to political stocks during the general elections of 2005, 2007 and 2011. The fourth offers conclusions and policy recommendations.

Inequalities in Wealth and Asset Holding

Economic inequality can be classified into two types: inequality of income, and inequality in wealth and assets.

In Thailand, income inequality is high, but wealth inequality is significantly higher (see Chapter 2). In 2006 the wealth of the richest 20 per cent of people was 70 times that of the poorest 20 per cent. According to the magazine *Money and Banking*, in 2010 the richest five thousand people came from around two hundred families. They held shares on the Stock Exchange of Thailand (SET) with a total value of 690 billion baht or 8.3 per cent of the total market value.[1]

At the end of November 2012, there were 1.2 million accounts of those who buy and sell shares on SET. Of these, 788,329 accounts buy and sell through security companies and 433,650 through the internet. The number of people involved is less than 1.2 million as many hold both types of accounts. Only 330,000 accounts had placed at least one order to buy and sell in the previous month. These active players represent only 0.5 per cent of the total population of 65.4 million. As most people perceive the capital market as a high risk investment, these 330,000 investors are probably drawn from the richest 20 per cent of the population.

One cause of the great inequality in wealth distribution is that Thai governments have never seriously taxed land or assets, but instead have often offered tax benefits that actively contribute to greater inequality. For example, in 2007 the government temporarily increased the amount of income exempted from tax if invested in a Retirement Mutual Fund or Long-term Equity Fund from 500,000 baht to 700,000 baht, even though the potential beneficiaries of this measure include only about 11,000 people with an annual net income of at least 4 million baht (see Chapter 9).

Policies and regulations (or non-regulations) for the capital market have a direct impact on inequality outside the market. Many research studies by financial economists have pointed out weaknesses inside the capital market, especially the issue of imperfect market information, which results in unequal market access, leading in turn to inefficiency in the allocation of financial resources in the whole economy and hence slower than optimum growth (Banerjee and Newman 1991; Aghion and Bolton 1997; Piketty 2014). Another factor contributing to inequality inside the market is political influence in cases where powerful people are either the major shareholders in listed companies or closely connected to them.

In addition, the globalization of finance, meaning the integration of stock and money markets across the world, has resulted in increased volatility which also contributes to inequality.

For example, in the US, the top 1 per cent of the population (with income over US$380,000 in 2008) has experienced more financial volatility since the early 1980s. When the economy booms, their incomes grow three times faster than the rest of the population. When the economy slumps, their incomes fall by two to three times more than the rest. Between 2007 and 2009, the number of Americans earning US$1 million and above fell by 40 per cent from around 400,000 to 236,888 persons, and their total income fell by half. The US Revenue Department found that changes in wealth are now linked to the capital market more than the macroeconomy. Stock prices are over 20 times more volatile than the rates of economic growth, resulting in rapid swings in the asset value of rich individuals.

As capital now skips across borders, asset bubbles can blow up rather quickly with larger and broader impact than in the past. The same is true of debt. Household debts of the richest 1 per cent in the US increased more than three times between 1989 and 2007 to US$600,000 million.

While Thai government policies on the capital market have contributed to economic inequality, the Thai capital market now faces many new challenges in financial globalization. Many in the financial sector have pressed the government to initiate reforms. A Committee on Thai Capital Market Development was formed in 2008 and stated its vision in a plan for 2009–13 as follows:

> Thai capital market is the major mechanism to mobilize, allocate, and monitor the efficient deployment of economic resources for the maximum benefit in developing the country's capability and potential to compete. (Committee on Thai Capital Market Development 2009)

Reducing inequality does not form any part of the vision or targets of the capital market plan.

Inequality and the Capital Market

Transactions in the capital market affect inequality in two ways, first between people in the market and those outside it, and second among those in the capital market between those who have access to inside information and those who do not. This study focuses on this latter issue.

Inequality Inside the Capital Market

According to the Securities and Exchange Act, "inside information" means "information material to changes in the prices of securities which has not yet been disclosed to the public and to which information he has access by virtue of his office or position."[2] Those with access to inside information tend to be market insiders including senior executives, directors, officials and professionals who work with share-issuing companies in roles such as auditors and investment bankers, along with officials of SET, officials in supervisory roles in government agencies, politicians, and some media persons.

Regulations on insider trading are an important part of measures to protect all investors against receiving false and misleading information. Investors depend on information that is correct and freely available. The regulations protect the "equal rights to information" among all investors. The argument against the use of inside information in stock trading states that equal access to information is needed to create share prices that are "efficient," meaning prices that reflect the financial position and performance of the company. If investors believe that share prices are not efficient, they will not invest for fear that they are disadvantaged compared to those who have inside information and who will reap gains at the expense of those without inside information.

According to the current oversight practice in the market, illegal use of inside information refers to buying and selling of shares by senior executives of listed companies who are likely to have secret information on the companies due to their official positions. In this definition, spouses are counted as "insiders." In some cases, it is difficult to determine what information qualifies as "inside information" that will affect share prices. Securities laws in Thailand and abroad thus require those in the inner circle of the market to make a daily report to the Securities and Exchange Commission (SEC) about their buying and selling of stocks of the companies in which they work. These reports are public information that other investors can use when making decisions about buying and selling.

Some oppose these regulations on grounds that use of inside information improves the efficiency of the market as it stimulates turnover, increases liquidity in the market, and provides incentives for executives and directors to invest in innovations and pay attention to their official duties. They argue that inside information should be seen as "rewards" or "incentives" with utility.

Those who support these regulations stress that insider trading enhances inequality between those with and without insider information by creating what amounts to an "economic rent."

Inequality Inside the Thai Capital Market

Inequality inside the Thai capital markets is caused by market imperfections, especially imperfect knowledge or information. Those with inside information have better opportunities to make more profits than those without. Inequality inside the capital market may be divided into four main types: inequality which arises from illegal practices; inequality which arises from practices that are not illegal but against SEC rules; inequality which arises from legal practices; inequality which arises from illegal practices involving figures with political power who are closely associated with major shareholders of a listed company. This section will consider the first three types, while the following section will focus on political stocks.

Inequality Arising from Illegal Practices

Dishonest actions tend to be committed by insiders who have inside information about listed companies. These persons may be shareholders, directors, and senior executives in the company, or others who have access to inside information through their duties as financial advisors, auditors, stock analysts, officials at SET and SEC, or media persons who are close to major shareholders.

Insiders seeking rent must depend on many collaborators. For example, those who want to "churn" a stock price upwards in order to lure buyers often hire or persuade others to collaborate with them in order to reduce the uncertainty of securing profit and to reduce the risk of being targeted for investigation. They may, for instance, induce the executives of the listed company to float false good news about the company, or induce the marketing staff of the company to disguise buying and selling via nominees.

Such dishonest actions to create rents in the capital market often offend against several clauses of the law at the same time, not only for the specific offence but also for window-dressing the accounts, failing to report ownership of shares, spreading false information and using accomplices.

Inequality Arising from Legal Practices against SEC Regulations

Disclosing inside information promptly so that investors have equal opportunity in the market is an important condition to reduce the inequality within the market. However, SEC and SET have not enforced the regulations concerning the disclosure of information efficiently and fairly. There is variation between listed and unlisted companies.

SEC reports information through an online system called SETSMART.[3] Kaohoon (meaning "stock news") is a popular website for stock news.[4] A study (Sarinee 2008) found differences in the way these two sources reported news about stocks that exhibited an irregular trading pattern (and were placed on the "Turnover List" according to SET rules). On Kaohoon 54 per cent of news about these stocks was published during the period of irregular trading, but on SETSMART only 31 per cent of the news about these stocks was published during that same period. This suggested that disclosure rules were not being effectively enforced, and that it is possible for company "insiders" to have significant advantage over other investors.

For 21 of the 27 stocks tracked in the study, half of the days when there was unusual trading in these stocks went unreported in either outlet. This means that most companies ignored the SEC rule that, when there is abnormal trading of stocks, listed companies must "consider whether there are rumors or other significant events on which the company should take action," and even if the company "does not know the cause of the abnormal trading," the company must "inform everyone that the company has no important development in the business or operation of the company other than information already given, to the best of the company's knowledge."

In the case of three companies with unusually active trading (ASP, PHATRA, and KEST),[5] the proportion of days with no reported news were 88, 85 and 75 per cent respectively. This suggests that SEC had been lenient or discriminatory in applying its own rules on disclosure for some listed companies who occupy almost half of the seats on the SEC board.

Enforcement of disclosure rules is clearly incomplete. There is still inequality between private media and the official media of SEC, and between a minority who has access to inside information and all other investors.

Inequality Arising from Practices That are Legal

The "inner circle" in listed companies, according to the SEC definition, encompasses all directors and senior executives, plus their spouses, who are in a better position to know information, both confidential and non-confidential, about a listed company than outsiders. Members of this "inner circle" are allowed to buy and sell shares in their own companies as long as they do not use inside information, and as long as they report such trading to SEC. This arrangement amounts to a reasonable compromise between the rights of those in the "inner circle" and the reduction of asymmetry of information in the capital market.

SEC specifies that those in the "inner circle" of listed companies must report changes in the share ownership of their companies within three days of the transaction. This is a very short period when compared to rules in other countries. In the US, for example, the report must be made by the 10th of the following month, meaning the lead-time may be up to 41 days (for a transaction made on the 1st of a month of 31 days). As a result, the timing of disclosure may affect a share price in the US, but in Thailand, the effect is not as significant due to a much shorter regulatory timeframe for reporting.

Many research studies in Thailand show this is true. However, insiders may still make unusual gains when compared to outsiders, even though outsiders have opportunities to follow suit in time. For example, Karuntarat, Seksak and Piman (2005), who used an event study model to analyze trading of securities by insiders of SET listed companies from 1993 to 1999, found that transactions by insiders increased steadily from 1993 to a peak in 2000, three years after the financial crisis, with most of the transactions being sales. Moreover, insiders were able to time their buy orders at the optimum moment, just before the stock prices rose (average abnormal return −AAR zero or negative), but made no abnormal gains on sales. Because the stocks offered opportunities for abnormal gains for as much as four to five days after the insider transaction, some outsiders were also able to make abnormal gains by following the insiders, but their gains were lower.

The upside of regulations requiring insiders to report their transactions is that the asymmetry in information between insiders and outsiders is reduced, but the downside is that insiders are incentivized to disguise their transactions by using the accounts of nominees so they can avoid reporting the trades to SEC. Sarinee (2006) found that as much as 21.4 per cent of all stocks are held by nominees. Some foreign nominees hold 10.4 per cent of 64 stocks that are rarely traded and make no dividend payments, and hence seem of no interest, leading to suspicions that these stocks are held on behalf of Thai investors who do not wish to reveal themselves.

The authorities should improve the definitions and regulations concerning the disclosure of the true identity of share owners, as the existing arrangements are full of loopholes.

A Case Study of Political Stocks

Inequality inside the capital market may also arise when those with political power are members or close associates of those with a major shareholding in listed companies. In capital markets in both developed and undeveloped countries all over the world, some shares are seen to move in response to major political events such as general elections in ways that contradict the random walk hypothesis. Umstead (1977), the first statistical study of this phenomenon published in a leading academic journal, linked stock movements in the US to the cycles of presidential elections, showing that from 1927 to 1974 the average returns on stocks was much higher in the eight quarters before a presidential election than in the eight quarters after the election.

Such empirical results were confirmed by several other studies, such as Allvine and O'Neill (1980), Huang (1985), Gartner and Wellershoff (1995), Hensel and Ziemba (1995), and Wong and McAleer (2007). Booth and Booth (2003) found that a pattern of stock movements keyed to the presidential election cycle can be traced from 1803 to the present.

Some researchers explain that share prices rise before elections because the governing party tries to boost the economy so that voters will feel contented, credit the governing party for their well-being, and vote the party back again. The governing party is also careful to avoid any unpopular measures in this period.

In Thailand, the link between share price movements and election cycles is also observable. Since the financial crisis of 1997, the movement has become more marked and the phenomenon has become part of "public wisdom." Before an election, stocks which are linked to politics (hereafter called "political stocks") are bought and sold in unusually large quantities and values.

In Thailand, political stocks account for a high proportion of the total stocks traded. When patrons of these companies have access to state power, they will give favors to them. Mara Faccio (2004) of Vanderbilt University, who studied political stocks in 47 countries, found that 42 per cent of stocks on SET were politically linked, and that Thailand ranked second in the world on this measure, beaten only by Russia (87 per cent).

Thai investors have long known that in the pre-election period political stocks will be active and the capital market as a whole will be bullish because of speculation on political stocks. Veteran investors believe

> the stock market is the bread and butter of political investors. When any group comes to power, it has an impact on businesses associated with political stocks including real estate, consumer goods, construction materials, and financial institutions.... In the past whenever any political group came to power, its power network will be favorable to businesses of its friends which receive direct assistance.... At the same time, profits are made indirectly, because the share prices of these listed companies rise and fall on news about the owners bidding for projects, or getting better business opportunities than others who do not have these political connections. These are ways to make good profits which can be invested back in politics for the future.[6]

Political stocks in Thailand are of three major types: (1) listed stocks of a state enterprise, or its subsidiary, or a joint venture in which a state enterprise has control, or a listed company in which the government is a major shareholder; (2) listed stocks of a company that receives its main income from concession businesses, or procuring materials for the government, or engaging in natural resource extraction under the control of the government; and (3) listed stocks of a company where those controlling the company are close to politicians or have relatives with political power.

Using ownership data from SET, public information on companies, reports on political donations to political parties, and interviews with brokers on SET, we identified 57 companies as political stocks under the above definition.

Research Methodology

The technique known as an "event study" analyses the impact of an event on a stock price by comparing the actual price to an estimate of what the price would have been had the event not taken place. The event could be an announcement about the company's performance, the passing of a new law, or whatever.

The estimated price is computed using econometric methods. The difference between the actual price and the estimated price is called an "abnormal return." The time is divided into three periods: the pre-event period; the event period; and the post-event period. The price in the pre-event period is used for calculating the estimated price during the event period. The abnormal return (AR) is calculated in the event period. In cases where an event occurs over more than one time period, the abnormal return is calculated cumulatively (cumulative abnormal return, CAR), and both AR and CAR are examined to test for statistical significance.

This study examines the impact of the results announced on election day on the prices of political stocks. This event affects all stocks (total clustering), hence the AR of each stock must be examined separately by using a dummy variable for the time of the election in order to isolate the statistical impact of the election on AR. The modeling of stock prices uses the Fama-French 3-Factor Model, which is popularly used because it has high explanatory power empirically, but a limitation that it has no clear theoretical basis. The significance (p value) of the dummy variable indicates whether a stock has an abnormal return during the event period.

This study uses daily data on stock prices from Datastream. Stock prices of the previous day may affect prices, because uncompleted orders can be carried over to the following day, hence the model also takes into consideration the returns to stocks on the previous day.

The study covers three general elections: February 6, 2005, won by the Thai Rak Thai Party, when Thaksin Shinawatra became prime minister; December 23, 2007, won by Palang Prachachon Party, when Samak Sundaravej became prime minister; and July 3, 2011, won by the Pheu Thai Party, when Yingluck Shinawatra became prime minister. Three versions of the event period were used, namely for 14, 17, and 20 days up to and including the election day respectively. As the analysis uses time series regression, the pre-event period was set at 200 days to give a large number of observations.

Study Results

The political stocks most likely to have abnormal returns in the election period are those of companies whose owners are relatives of those with political power. In all, 67 per cent of stocks of this type had an abnormal return. Next came the companies whose controllers are close to political heavyweights, where the proportion was 40 per cent. Next came stocks of companies where the owners are close associates of politicians in the winning party, where the proportion was 38 per cent. Next are stocks of companies which are clients of the government or obtain concessions from government, where the proportion was 25 per cent. The category of political stocks with the lowest proportion of abnormal returns (23 per cent) was state enterprises or their subsidiaries or joint ventures.

In all cases the abnormal returns were positive (price higher than estimated). This shows that stock speculation linked to election results is focused on companies associated with the party anticipated (correctly) to win.

This further suggests that investors in these political stocks anticipate future benefits from companies that are associated with the winning party, and that these benefits (in terms of abnormal returns) are greater than the loss for political stocks associated with the losing party.

The level of abnormal returns was higher in 2011 than in 2005 and 2007. Possibly investors were more confident about which party would win, or the party had amassed a bigger war chest in advance of the election. However, the event study cannot distinguish whether speculation or a bigger war chest was the key factor.

The rise in the average return to all political stocks between the pre-event period and the event period was very large: 960 per cent compared to −79 per cent in 2005; 572 per cent compared to −10 per cent in 2007, and 2,330 per cent compared to 144 per cent in 2011. Investors thus had opportunities to reap much greater gains than in normal times, providing incentives for speculation in these political stocks.

Conclusions and Recommendations

There is some good news. The new trend of stock trading via internet together with the liberalization of trading fees has reduced the cost of participating in the market. Even though insiders in the Thai capital market can obtain abnormal returns from stock trading, outsiders can benefit at a slightly lower level by following the example of the insiders.

The gap between insiders and outsiders is small because insiders have to report their changes in stock ownership within three days, a much shorter time than in many other countries. However, this rule may tempt insiders to disguise themselves by using nominees for stock trading to avoid reporting. The current regulations on disclosure of traders' true identity do not prevent such use of nominees.

The enforcement of rules and regulations concerning fairness in the capital market has become more stringent. In 2011 SEC imposed fines on 24 cases of using insider information to fix a share price, and charged another 12 cases, the highest numbers seen in the past 12 years. However, in accordance with the criminal code, cases about churning stock prices have to be proved "beyond doubt," which is difficult and time-consuming. SEC and SET have not enforced the Freedom of Information Act in the capital market equitably and seriously.

Our study of the impact of elections showed clearly that substantial abnormal returns could be gained, especially by speculating on stocks of companies where the owners are kin or close associates of the party likely to win the election.

Some government policies aggravate inequality inside the capital market. For example, there is no capital gains tax, and income from stock trading has been exempted from income tax in order to promote saving and investment in the stock market. A capital gains tax could be designed in such a way as not to affect small investors or long-term investment.

Inequality in capital markets is often caused by people with insider information or with political connections who make use of the market to create and capture economic rents that are then used for election campaigns. Authorities cannot easily distinguish between those manipulating political stocks for political purposes and those merely speculating on the outcome of the election.

Reducing inequality of this sort requires the development and efficient enforcement of relevant laws and regulations. Many countries have achieved this. For Thailand the following are some recommendations.

Prohibit Those with Political Power from Using Insider Information

This can be achieved by expanding the definition of "insider" in section 241 of the Securities and Exchange Act to include those with political power such as MPs, senators, and members of independent bodies. This reform would follow practice in many countries, such as the recent Stop Trading on Congressional Knowledge Act (STOCK Act for short) of April 2012 in the USA, which prohibits congressmen as well as senior officials of the executive from using "non-public information" obtained in their work to assist their stock trading. These persons must report any stock trading within 45 days, rather than within a year as under previous rules, and their trades are made public on a government website.

Amend the Law to Increase the Civil Power of SEC

At present any wrongdoing under the Securities and Exchange Act is a criminal offence, which requires a long process governed by the criminal code. This is not suitable for complex fraud cases in capital markets. The government should amend the law to give SEC semi-judicial powers to impose penalties for civil offences. This would give SEC more flexibility in enforcing the law than in the past, as well as allowing offenders to pay hefty fines in return for not having to admit guilt, as practiced internationally in the enforcement of securities exchange laws. (This proposal was included in the Capital Market Development Plan 2009–13, but is not yet realized.)

In addition, the government should improve the mechanisms by which investors may file a case for damages so that small investors might use the mechanism more easily and at less cost. A class action law should be passed urgently. An act was drafted by SEC in 1999 and forwarded to the Council of State, but the draft has never been submitted to parliament. (This also was in the Capital Market Development Plan 2009–13.)

Improve Regulations on the True Identity of Stock Holders

At present the use of nominees to hold shares is very common. Politicians use nominees when they want to raise money for political purposes, and others use nominees when churning stocks. The burden of proving who are the real owners falls on investigating officials, and proof is very difficult. The government should amend the definition of related persons in section 258 of the Securities and Exchange Act to cover both "nominees" and "real owners." The model could be the US Securities Exchange Act 1934, which requires owners of more than 5 per cent of the stock of a listed company to report the true owner and give evidence of the sale. The "true owner" is defined by these principles: (a) any person who directly or indirectly has the right to vote and/or control over the investment, including the power to sell or transfer it; (b) any person who uses a trust, proxy, power of attorney, benefit sharing agreement, or any agreement that separates the stock from the true owner in order to evade reporting, has the duty to include all those stocks as under the ownership of the true owner; (c) the calculation and reporting of any owner's stocks must include those that the person has the right to obtain within 60 days such as by custodian/escrow agreements, warrants, conversion of stocks, dissolution of a trust, or other agreements.

The US Securities Exchange Act 1934 also requires true owners with more than 5 per cent ownership to make public the information as follows: their identity, address, citizenship and objectives of holding the stocks; the source of money to buy the stocks, including the true identity of creditors other than a commercial bank under the regulation of the government; any plans to sell assets, merge businesses, or make major changes in executive and management structures to control the business; the amounts of stocks owned or with rights to own, either directly or indirectly (such as warrants, stock option, etc.); and details of any contracts or agreements about matters such as stock transfers, joint ventures, profit sharing, or use of proxies.

The government should also amend the Securities and Exchange Act to allow listed companies and small stockowners who own altogether more than 0.5 per cent of the total stocks to demand that large stockholders (with more than 5 per cent of the total stocks) show proof of their true identity, and to allow SEC to abrogate the rights of those that fail to comply within the time limit. In the UK, a listed company may stop paying dividends or other compensation until a share owner provides proof of true ownership.

Increase Penalties to be Comparable to Other Countries in the Region

At the moment, penalties for distributing false information or deceiving other investors are the lowest among countries in the region.

Country	Penalty for disseminating false information or deceiving other investors
Thailand	Jail for not more than 2 years and/or fine of not more than twice the benefits received or to be received, but not less than 500,000 baht.
Philippines	Jail for not less than 7 years and no more than 21 years, and/or fine of not less than 50,000 peso (about 36,000 baht), and not more than 500,000 peso (about 3.6 million baht).
Malaysia	Jail for not more than 10 years, and fine of not less than 1 million ringgit (about 9.9 million baht).
Hong Kong	In a criminal case, jail for not more than 10 years and fine of not less than HK$10 million (about 46 million baht). In a civil case, jail for not more than 10 years and fine of not more than HK$ 1 million (about 4.6 million baht). The court may ban the offender from being an investor or executive of a listed company for five years.
Singapore	Jail for not more than 7 years, and/or fine not more than twice the benefits received or to be received, but not less than S$230,000 (about 5.8 million baht).
Taiwan	Jail between from 3 to 10 years, and fine of T$10–200 million (about 11–220 million baht).
South Korea	Jail for not more than 10 years, or fine not more than 3 times the benefits received or 20 million won (about 770,000 baht), whichever is higher. If the benefits received are valued at 500–5,000 million won (19–190 million baht), the offender may be jailed for not less than 3 years. If the benefits received are over 5,000 million won (about 190 million baht), the offender may be jailed for not less than 5 years.

Increase Efficiency in Enforcement

In the last few years (2012–13), SEC has been more serious about imposing fines for using insider information to churn stocks, as shown by the rising value of fines levied. However, SET and SEC should be more stringent in cases where there is reason to suspect that stocks are being churned though there is not enough information to identify those responsible.

For example, in cases where a stock's prices show unusual movements for several days in succession, and the media report rumors of churning, SEC should force the company in question to report to SEC that "according to the company's knowledge there is no reason why the trading of the company's stocks should differ from the normal state of the market," in line with SEC's current rules of disclosure. SEC should also warn the media that they may be distributing false information, which is against the Securities and Exchange Act. This will let all investors know indirectly that this stock price is moving abnormally, and force the company and the media to be more accountable for propagating information that has an impact on share prices.

Tailpiece

In one of the few studies of the Thai stock market, Handley (2014: 97) detailed the "intense politicization, rooted in vested interests, of both capital market development and state enterprise privatization." That was two decades ago. There have been many improvements, but Handley's basic insight remains true. As noted in Chapters 1 and 2, the ownership of financial assets in Thailand is highly concentrated, and only the wealthy have access to the potentially higher gains from the capital market. Rather few people invest in the stock market in part because they perceive that the market is too risky and not fair. It is difficult to avoid the conclusion that loose regulation persists because certain parties benefit. In this respect, the stock market is simply one example of an economic institution where rigging the operations in favor of a few works to the disadvantage of the many.

Notes

1. "Announcing 2010 Stock Tycoons: Thongma Vijitpongpun Champion." *Manager Online*, Dec. 12, 2010. Available at http://www.manager.co.th/iBizChannel/ViewNews.aspx?NewsID=9550000150665.

2. Clause 241 of English translation at http://www.sec.or.th/EN/SECInfo/
    LawsRegulation/Documents/actandroyal/1Securities.pdf.
3. An acronym for SET Market Analysis and Reporting Tool, a fee-based
    service which claims to "seamlessly integrate comprehensive sources of
    Thai listed company data, that is, historical stock prices, historical in-
    dices, listed company profile and historical news. By using SETSMART,
    the investors will have an alternative investment tool to access the same
    channel of information like those Professionals." It has both English and
    Thai versions. See www.setsmart.com.
4. Kaohoon presents stock news rather like a wire service, only in Thai
    language. See www.kaohoon.com.
5. These are the stock market acronyms for: Asia Plus Group Holdings
    Securities, a leading securities trader; the Phatra Financial Group, since
    absorbed into Kiatnikin Phatra Financial Group; and Kim Eng Securi-
    ties Thailand, since absorbed into Maybank Kim Eng.
6. "Political Stocks Rally before being Butchered," *Manager Online*, June
    24, 2007. Available at http://www.manager.co.th/Daily/ViewNews.
    aspx?NewsID=9500000073408.

References

Aghion, P. and Bolton, P. 1997. "A Theory of Trickle-Down Growth and
    Development." *Review of Economic Studies* 64, 2: 151–72.
Allvine, F.C. and D.E. O'Neill. 1980. "Stock Market Returns and the Presi-
    dential Cycle: Implications for Market Efficiency." *Financial Analysts
    Journal* 36: 49–56.
Banerjee, Abhijit V. and Newman, Andrew F. 1991. "Risk-Bearing and
    the Theory of Income Distribution," *Review of Economic Studies* 58, 2
    (April): 211–35.
Barro, Robert J. 1999. "Inequality, Growth, and Investment." National Bu-
    reau of Economic Research Working Paper No. 7038, March.
Karuntarat Boonyawat, Seksak Jumreornvong and Piman Limpaphayom.
    2005. *Insider Trading: Evidence from Thailand.* Available at http://www.
    thammasatreview.tu.ac.th/tu_doc/2005-Volume10-No1/3[1][1].insider_
    trading-revise.pdf.
Booth, J.R. and L.C. Booth. 2003. "Is the Presidential Cycle in Security Re-
    turns Merely a Reflection of Business Conditions?" *Review of Financial
    Economics* 12: 131–59.
Committee on Thai Capital Market Development. 2009. "Phaen phatthana
    talat thun thai pho so 2552–2556" [Capital Market Development Plan
    2009–13]. Available at http://www.set.or.th/th/about/vision/files/CMP_
    Master.pdf.
Faccio, Mara. 2004. "Politically Connected Firms." Available at http://ssrn.
    com/abstract=444960 or http://dx.doi.org/10.2139/ssrn.444960.

Gartner, M. and Klaus W. Wellershoff. 1995. "Is There an Election Cycle in American Stock Returns?" *International Review of Economics and Finance* 4, 4: 387–410.

Handley, Paul M. 1997. "More of the Same? Politics and Business, 1987–96." In *Political Change in Thailand: Democracy and Participation*, ed. Kevin Hewison. London and New York: Routledge, pp. 94–113.

Hensel, Chris R. and Ziemba, William T. 1995. "The January Barometer." *The Journal of Investing* 4, 2 (Summer): 67–70.

Huang, R.D. 1985. "Common Stock Returns and Presidential Elections." *Financial Analysts Journal* 41: 58–61.

Piketty, Thomas. 2014. *Capital in the Twenty-First Century*. Cambridge, MA: Belknap Press of Harvard University Press.

Sarinee Achavanuntakul. 2006. "Kan chai tua thaen thoe hun (nomini) nai talat laksap haeng prathet thai" [Use of Nominee Shareholders in SET]. TDRI Conference on Transparency in Good Governance: Issues Arising from the Shin Corp Sale.

————. 2008. "Kan phatthana talat kan ngoen phuea jaroen toep to thang sethakit korani sueksa khaosan nai talat thun" [Development of the Capital Market for Economic Development: Case Study of Information in the Stockmarket]. TDRI annual conference.

Umstead, David A. 1997. "Forecasting Stock Market Prices." *Journal of Finance* 32, 2 (May): 427–41.

Wilkinson, Richard and Kate Pickett. 2009. *The Spirit Level: Why More Equal Societies Almost Always Do Better*. London: Allen Lane.

Wong Wing-Keung and Michael McAleer. 2007. "Non-Trading Day Effects in Asymmetric Conditional and Stochastic Volatility Models." *Econometrics Journal* 10, 1: 113–23.

5

Elite Networking through Special Executive Courses

Nualnoi Treerat and Parkpume Vanichaka[1]

The class that assembled for the first time in Bangkok in March 2010 was not an average group of freshmen students. To begin with, there was Banharn Silpa-archa, a former prime minister and 40-year veteran of parliamentary politics who, at age 77, was hardly in the usual catchment for education. Beside him on the school benches were five other former ministers, one who had also been commander-in-chief of the army, two other generals, two deputy police chiefs, the head and two deputy heads of major government agencies, and a sprinkling of judges and MPs. In a class of less than a hundred students, this concentration of the powerful could not have happened by random chance. Nor was this an ancient and prestigious seat of learning. The school had been founded only five years earlier, and the vast majority of Thailand's population had never heard of it. The reason why this school's benches groaned under the weight of so much power had little to do with the content of the coursework or the value of the certificate received on graduation. Rather, it had everything to do with networking. These powerful people were there because the others were too.

In the past two decades, several key institutions have begun to offer short courses that nominally offer training for senior executives from various sectors of society but in reality exist primarily to create networks across the elites of the society. These courses attract people from the bureaucracy, military, judiciary, politics, media and business. Their motivation to enroll has less to do with the expertise they gain from coursework and more to do with the relationships they develop through the class and the alumni association. Several people have attended many of these classes. Enrolments are oversubscribed.

How important are these new quasi-schools in creating networks among influential people, and what are the political implications? This chapter examines the process of elite networking in six executive courses. The first part examines the origins of these courses, and the second looks at their course content and networking activities. The third examines a sample network in depth, and looks at the benefits for the students and the parent institutions. The fourth section notes the prominence of billionaires among those attending these courses, and the final section looks at this phenomenon from a political economy perspective.

The Demand for Networks

The relatively low level of institutionalization in Thai public life has been noted many times—from the Cornell anthropologists' notion of "loose structure" in the 1950s through to Danny Unger's work on limited social capital in the 1990s (Embree 1950; Unger 1998). The monarchy, military, and bureaucracy are the only organizations with both structure and historical depth. Parliament has been constantly disrupted. With only one exception, political parties are ephemeral. Business associations have only very recently acquired more weight. The very rapid pace of economic and social change in recent decades has also meant that institution building lags behind social realities. In this situation, informal relations play a major role. Decision making often evolves from informal processes, while the formal institutions often merely act as a rubber stamp. Informal relations operate through *khwam pen phuak phong*, literally just "being a group together," meaning that such informal relations can be engineered among people who have no prior relations of kinship or friendship. Anek Laothammatas noticed that

> Thai society…has to make use of private networks. Those good at politics must have many networks…those who join various groups must be easy-going, approachable—so that group formation proceeds very casually based mainly on friendship giving rise to mutual trust. (Interview, Jan. 22, 2010)

The original model for these new networks came from the alumni associations of the major universities. Until the 1960s, most recruits into Thailand's elite, other than its military component, passed through a handful of schools and either one or the other of the country's first two universities, Chulalongkorn and Thammasat. Social bonds among students were cemented by hazing rituals, sports, and other campus activities. Alumni associations were formed to preserve these bonds into later life. The resulting networks, particularly those focused on certain faculties (such as Chulalongkorn University's Faculty of Political Science), were important in the relatively narrow social and political elite of the time, especially in the bureaucracy (Likhit 1978: 121–51).

The military adopted and also modified this model. Classmates at the Chulachomklao Military Academy and the Cadet School were encouraged to form strong lateral ties, and to preserve these ties through alumni activities in subsequent years. As a result, by the 1980s, the class groups of certain years had become players in the internal politics of the military. Most famously, alumni of Class Five of the Military Academy were responsible for the coup of 1991.

In 1955, the military founded the National Defense College (*Witthayalai pongkan ratcha-anajak*, Wo Po Or) to give short-course training to civilians in order to instill in their minds the importance of national security and the role of the military. Classes included both military officers and outsiders, mainly civilian bureaucrats. In 1967, the catchment was expanded to include executives of state enterprises. Besides its role as a propaganda vehicle for the military, this institution gradually became important also for building informal links out from the military into newly important social groups. In 1988, the military created a new institution to accelerate the development of this networking, the National Security Academy for Government and Private Sector (Po Ro Or). At the time, the military's role in the polity was coming under increasing attack from business quarters. A burning issue was the complaint that the military budget was eating into the regular annual budgets, which should have been used for projects to support industries and other businesses. Po Ro Or primarily recruited students from business and other civil society groups.

At these military courses, the educational content was less important than the active encouragement of bonding and networking. Much class work was in groups. Classes made many trips and visits, both within Thailand and overseas, offering long periods for socialization. Contact at the classroom was supplemented on the golf course and in exclusive clubs and karaoke parlors. Bonds formed during the course were sustained by an active round of alumni activities. Most importantly, these academies actively inculcated the military culture of unconditional commitment to help colleagues in every possible way. Refusing a request from an old class member would be "bad form."

These military courses were initially highly successful. Many of the most prominent businessmen of the era joined the classes. So too did many high fliers in the civilian bureaucracy and some select members of the media and civil society. The resulting links were vital in bridging the gaps separating military, civilian, business and professional groups. For two decades, there was scarcely a major figure in Thai public life (outside of royalty) that had not attended one of these programs.

After the political crisis of 1991–92, when the army took power by coup but was later forced from power by street demonstrations, the prestige of the military was badly damaged, and its role in national politics sharply reduced. The attraction of the military courses consequently declined. Moreover, changes in the power structure of the country created a demand to extend this network model to embrace newly emerging nodes of power. The absolute dominance of narrow elites in the civilian and military bureaucracy had diminished as new political forces developed. The bureaucracy itself had expanded in size and complexity, particularly with the addition of new technocratic functions. Business groups had become richer and more politically established. Provincial centers had risen in importance, and their business elites had been drawn into national society by improved communications.

These changes created a demand for new network-building bodies. From the late 1990s, five new quasi-schools were launched on the model of the military academies.

1. In 1996, the Office of the Judiciary launched a "Senior Judicial Officers Course."
2. The King Prajadhipok Institute (KPI), founded in 1998 in the wake of the 1991–92 political crisis with the aim of promoting democracy through research and educational activities among the public at large and among politicians themselves, launched a "Course on Politics and Administration under Democracy for Executives" for MPs along with officials, businessmen and members of civil society groups.

3. In 2005 the Stock Exchange of Thailand (SET) created the Capital Market Academy (CMA) offering two executive courses a year on the capital market.
4. In 2008 the Chamber of Commerce created the Commerce Academy offering a "Top Executive Program in Commerce and Trade" (TEPCoT).
5. In 2009 the Election Commission created an Institute for Development of Politics and Elections offering a "High-level Course on the Development of Politics and Elections."

In addition, in 2003, the military opened up the courses at the National Defense College to politicians.

Of these six courses, four are organized by state institutions and two by private-sector bodies. All six have proved popular among executives from the public and private sectors. Several people have applied to enroll in more than one course. The principal attraction is not the course content but the opportunity to become part of networks of influential people spanning the bureaucracy, military, politics and business.

The Content and Character of Executive Courses

By 2011, a total of 6,921 persons had graduated from the National Defense College course, 857 from that of the Office of the Judiciary, 1,517 from the KPI course, 245 from that of the Election Commission, 1,039 from the Stock Exchange's CMA, and 285 from the Chamber of Commerce's TEPCoT. Tables 5.1 and 5.2 show the breakdown of the students in 2011.

The courses offered by the four public-sector bodies have an academic character and aim to develop capacities and impart information. They are also designed to promote networking and connections, but with no particular agenda. These institutions have been criticized for allowing students to use third parties to attend class and to carry out the research projects required as part of the assessment.

The two private-sector courses also have academic content. For example, the CMA course is divided under three headings: knowledge about the capital market, 50 per cent; corporate governance, 25 per cent; and leadership roles and social responsibility, 25 per cent. The content is largely technical, and the sessions are led by experts in the

Table 5.1 Breakdown of Students at Four Public-Sector Courses, 2011

	National Defense College		Office of the Judiciary		King Prajadhipok Institute		Election Commission	
	total	per cent	total	per cent	total	per cent	total	per cent
Business, financial	3	1.0	0	0.0	2	2.0	0	0.0
Business, non-financial	61	20.0	36	32.7	30	30.0	16	20.0
Politicians	6	2.0	2	1.8	3	3.0	31	38.8
Bureaucracy/state enterprise	83	27.2	11	10.0	21	21.0	12	15.0
Military	112	36.7	6	5.5	11	11.0	2	2.5
Police	13	4.3	6	5.5	1	1.0	1	1.3
Judicial	12	3.9	30	27.3	12	12:0	4	5.0
NGO	7	2.3	3	2.7	4	4.0	5	6.3
Media	0	0.0	2	1.8	0	0.0	2	2.5
Academic/education	1	0.3	6	5.5	4	4.0	1	1.3
Other	7	2.3	8	7.3	12	12.0	6	7.5
Total	305	100.0	110	100.0	100	100.0	80	100.0

Table 5.2   Breakdown of Students at Two Private-Sector Courses, 2011

	CMA		TEPCoT	
	total	*per cent*	*total*	*per cent*
Business, financial	10	10.4	2	2.2
Business, non-financial	53	55.2	43	47.3
Politicians	5	5.2	1	1.1
Bureaucracy/state enterprise	11	11.5	23	25.3
Military	1	1.0	6	6.6
Police	3	3.1	1	1.1
Judicial	5	5.2	4	4.4
NGO	2	2.1	2	2.2
Media	0	0.0	2	2.2
Academic/education	2	2.1	3	3.3
Other	4	4.2	4	4.4
Total	96	100.0	91	100.0

field. Participants have to present a final project paper in order to qualify for a certificate of achievement. However, the course content and assessment conditions in the private-sector courses are much lighter and less burdensome than in the public-sector courses. In addition, these courses stress three other aspects: building a consensus among class members; promoting policy-making ideas that emerge from the class; and cementing relations among the students as a network that can act as a lobby for policy change.

All six institutions give importance to building close social relations among the members, using similar methods with minor variation in methods of recruitment, techniques for building relationships, and devices for sustaining these relationships after graduation.

Recruitment

The public-sector courses are open for application. The managers choose the students within a framework of quotas for different groups. While the private-sector courses also are open for applications, the managers invite targeted individuals to join the courses.

Qualifications. All six courses specify that members must be senior executives or prominent public figures in some field, and impose no requirement for prior knowledge or qualifications relating to the course content. The most important qualification is being some-one of accepted influence in society, economy or politics. In cases where applications exceed the course capacity, personal connections between the applicants and those on the selection committee are the next most important factor deciding whether an applicant will gain admission.

Size and structure of the class. All of these classes quickly became oversubscribed, resulting in expansion of class sizes. For example, the TEPCoT course grew from 37 students on its first intake to 91 by the fourth year. In most cases, courses initially favored applicants who were "owners and allies," meaning they came from institutions in fields closely allied to that of the course's parent institution (that is, finance-related firms and government agencies in the case of CMA), but these were rapidly outnumbered by "outsiders" from totally un-related fields, thus increasing the utility of these courses as the focus of broad-based networking.

Motivation of applicants. The principal motive of applicants is to participate in power networks, while the knowledge gained is sec-ondary. A course that is known to have alumni who are powerful or prominent in society, a relatively light academic burden, and broad selection criteria will be more popular than one with opposite charac-teristics. The popularity of the CMA is testament to this fact. The Chamber of Commerce followed the same strategy but was less suc-cessful at attracting politicians.

The CMA course was particularly successful in attracting many figures that were powerful and socially prominent. As a result, those joining these courses could hope for immediate benefit from the con-nections they thus gained. The National Security Academy targeted "rising stars" in the middle ranks of any organization, and their courses lasted a year. Members thus had to invest a long time in study, and face a delay before their class-fellows reached the levels of real power and influence—with a risk that they might not reach such a level at all. By contrast, the CMA courses were half the length, and the networking benefits more immediate and less subject to risk.

Building Relationships During the Course

Course managers arrange freshman inductions to "create familiarity and break down barriers" before the start of the course. In the Office of the Judiciary courses, this process extends over two days. Some courses eject the students who fail to attend this session. One student who attended the KPI's "Happy Freshman Induction" at a Pattaya hotel in February 2011 described the activities as follows:

> On the afternoon of 10 February, there were contact groups…making acquaintance among members of the Class 15, singing, clasping hands and embracing, exchanging names, the likes of each member, playing a "love bridge" game, playing competitive games such as tearing an A4 sheet into as long a strip as possible, cheering the group, and so on.
>
> I understood that KPI wanted to emphasize building as broad relations as possible. In particular in the "love bridge" game each participant, all of whom are "big" in their various bodies, must lose their "bigness" in order to create a cooperative and harmonious atmosphere for the task of building and maintaining a love bridge that is as secure and steady as possible.[2]

All six executive courses have a similar approach involving class-room discussion, debates, seminars, students taking turns to make presentations, and group projects. These methods oblige all the students to develop close working relationships with their classmates. For example, a handout for a TEPCoT class noted that the syllabus "emphasized learning through discussion and exchange of information, opinions, and true experience among class members rather than the transfer of information from a teacher." One student at the first year of this course explained the impact of this teaching method:

> TEPCoT is very good project that organizes classes by having the senior executive from each organization present and exchange their experiences, especially in group discussions, bringing true experience to discuss, giving new and different perspective, and building a net-work between government and the private sector. In addition, there is an exchange of opinions between the senior executives of each organization, creating understanding about the working style and limitations of different organizations, making it possible to work together with greater efficiency in the future.[3]

At the CMA, all members of the class address each other as *phi*, the form of address normally used to address someone of greater seniority. This practice is probably copied from the National Defense College, where it is not so strange since the age range of students is rather limited (48 to 53). But in the CMA classes, students range from

30 to 90 years, with those from government backgrounds tending to be older, and those from business tending to be younger. The use of the single form of address is a way of breaking down the social distance usually resulting from difference of age. CMA places great emphasis on "becoming friends" and "understanding one another and working together." One CMA activity is a "leadership camp" for developing local leaders in the provincial areas which doubles as an opportunity for tightening relations among the class members.

The CMA's thrice-a-week coursework is conducted in a building conveniently situated next to a prestigious golf course in the Bangkok inner suburbs. Many participants make a day (and night) of it by playing a round of golf with classmates in the morning, capping that with a sociable lunch, proceeding from the class to a group dinner, and continuing for karaoke until late in the night.

A CMA class is divided up into eight groups, each with no more than 12 members, selected to have a varied mix of backgrounds, age, and experience. Besides the classwork, there is a constant program of extracurricular activities, particularly involving opportunities for eating together. CMA has an "Evening Program" with the stated objective of "tightening relationships among the students in the same class which is an important component of the class to develop relationships among members of the group and between groups."[4] As part of the program there is a dinner after class every Thursday evening, with each group in the class taking turns to play host, decide upon a theme for the food, drink, music, and entertainment, and pick up the expenses. Each group competes to please the whole class as much as possible, and the private-sector class members are expected to be "big-hearted" in this activity. In CMA class 9, the cost of each of these evenings exceeded a million baht, since, as one participant observed, "there are a lot of private sector members and few government officials. Those with the ability are big-hearted and want to service their friends."[5]

Apart from these weekly activities, every CMA student has to participate in an annual event in which the alumni of all previous years welcome the current year's intake, with both the alumni and the new intake putting on a show. This event is especially important for cementing the relations within the class, as well as building links across classes. As one alumnus noted, "We had to prepare to put on a show for all the earlier alumni to watch, and we quickly became close during the rehearsals."[6] Each class also has several short trips and at least one (optional) overseas tour of seven to ten days (for example, to see the stock exchanges in New York and Tokyo), providing opportunity for extended socialization. These extra-curricular activities ensure that participants are able to build strong personal relationships within the four-month period of the course.

To create relations between classes at CMA, each student has a code number, and the alumni from previous classes are tasked to look after those in subsequent classes who have the same code. Whereas the classes from the military academies sometimes became competitors in military and national politics, CMA actively encourages vertical links between classes, as well as the horizontal ties among each class's members.

In addition, members of the CMA class initiated other activities for building relations among themselves, such as sporting contests (golf, football, futsal) within the class, and between classes, tourist trips, and eating together on various occasions. Such activities showed that relations among class members had reached a point where they no longer needed a third party to organize their joint activities. A former under-secretary at the Ministry of Communications commented, "We became very friendly, very close, very harmonious. Just recently our CMA class went on a trip together to the Maldives. Great fun. All my family went along too."[7]

Sustaining Relationships Beyond the Course

Any educational institution that wants to cultivate relations among its former students founds an alumni association. The fact that all of the executive courses have created alumni clubs or associations indicates that networking is a key objective of these courses.

These alumni bodies organize a regular stream of activities such as annual gatherings, freshman receptions, seminars, entertainments, sports events, and charitable activities in order to sustain contact among the alumni. For example, the alumni of the KPI course organized a concert to celebrate the 7th cycle birthday of the King on December 5, 2011. The alumni association of the National Defense College has a scheme for members to get discounts on goods and services from participating companies.

These alumni bodies also sometimes have a political role. For example, on January 31, 2012 the KPI alumni issued a statement on the proposed amendment of article 112 of the criminal code concerning lèse majesté. The CMA alumni prepared a plan for the development of the Thai capital market and presented it to the Ministry of Finance in February 2008. CMA class 11 prepared a plan entitled "National strategic plan for disseminating knowledge on finance to the public," which resulted in a joint scheme of the Stock Exchange of Thailand and the Bangkok Metropolitan Authority to have teaching on the capital market in 436 city schools.[8]

Apart from the alumni association activities, certain class members organize occasional dinners or meetings on various occasions such as a housewarming, celebrating a promotion, a golf game, or just an excuse to dine together. Such gatherings tend to take place among members of the same year, or a group within that year, and tend to be for fun rather than any social purpose.

Networking

Some students rarely take part in the alumni activities and make little use of the connections formed in these classes. But the fact that many high-status individuals are interested in joining the CMA classes indicates that they hope to gain some benefit from networking. Interviews with several class-members showed that personal relations between members of two different bodies resulted in a more efficient working relationship, with benefits for the institutions involved.

Some impression of the span of these networks can be gained by looking in more detail at the example of one general who attended these courses.

General A studied in three executive courses: at the National Security Academy class 4 in 1991: the CMA class 4 in 2007; and TEPCoT class 2 in 2009. General A had formerly been important in the army, had served in the senate, been a director of several major state enterprises, and director in several private companies—sometimes together with other classmates. The members of General A's network are here identified by the post they held at the time of study, or their current or most recent position in the case of the National Security Academy.

National Security Academy class 4, 1991

Director-general of the Department of General Education
National chief of police

Deputy commander-in-chief of the army
Minister of defense
Under-secretary, Ministry of Culture
Under-secretary, Ministry of Health
Director, Thai Beverage Company (Chang Beer)
Director and secretary, Chaipattana Foundation[9]
Member of the National Economic and Social Advisory Council
Chairman of the Board, Electricity Generating Authority of Thailand
Director-general, Department of Special Investigations, Royal Thai
    Police
Deputy under-secretary, Ministry of Foreign Affairs
National chief of police
Minister of finance
Chairman of the Board, Bangkok Rubber Company
Deputy governor of Bangkok
Deputy chairman, National Olympic Committee
Deputy managing director, Bangkok Entertainment (TV channel)
Chairman of the board, Trinity Finance Company

CMA class 4, 2007

Director, Siam Commercial Bank
Chairman, Siam Commercial Securities
Governor, Electricity Generating Authority of Thailand
Under-secretary, Ministry of Education
Rector, University of the Thai Chamber of Commerce
Deputy president, Court of Appeal
Deputy chairman of the board, Matichon Publishing (newspapers
    and books)
Under-secretary, Ministry of Energy
Deputy secretary-general, Office of the Narcotics Control Board
Chairman, Kim Eng Securities Thailand
Auditor, Ministry of Finance
Chairman of the board, Sahaviriya Steel
Chairman of the board, Stock Exchange of Thailand
Deputy secretary-general, Securities and Exchange Commission
Chairman and managing director, Cho Kanchang Construction
Deputy commissioner of police
Secretary of the parliament
Chairman of the Thai-Myanmar Friendship Association

Director and senior managing director, Charoen Pokphand (CP)
    Group
Director, TKS Technology (printing)
Chairman of the board, Institute of Economic Policy, Ministry of
    Finance
Director, Siam Piwat Company (real estate developer)

TEPCoT class 2, 2009

Director, Siam Commercial Bank
Managing director, Mitrphol Sugar
Director-general, Department of International Economics, Ministry
    of Foreign Affairs
Under-secretary, Ministry of Industry
Deputy under-secretary, Ministry of Commerce
Former under-secretary, Ministry of Communication
Director-general, Department of International Trade, Ministry of
    Commerce
Deputy chairman of the board, Matichon Publishing
Director-general, Customs Department
Deputy director, Committee on State Enterprise Policy, Ministry of
    Finance
President, Thai Chamber of Commerce
Secretary-general, Securities and Exchange Commission
Deputy under-secretary, Ministry of Agriculture
Director-general, Department of International Trade Negotiations,
    Ministry of Commerce
President, Appeals Court Zone 6
Presiding judge, Central Labor Court
Acting commissioner of police
Consultant, National Defense College
Director-general, Department of Alternative Energy Development,
    Ministry of Energy
Deputy under-secretary, Ministry of Commerce
Deputy director-general, Tax Department
Under-secretary, Ministry of Commerce
Director, King Prajadhipok Institute
Deputy attorney-general
Chairman of the Board, ICC International (brandname goods, Central
    group)

The Ties that Bind

Most graduates see that the major benefits of attending CMA are the number, variety, and quality of the links that they are able to establish in such a short space of time:

> As for learning, it may be better to spend time reading for yourself. But from the social perspective, the program is wonderful. It's good for building connections for information and support.... The ties that bind are mutual interests.
>
> Business people benefit in the long run. Meeting politicians such as ministers gives them connections. When someone from their class is in government, they have connections to some extent, creating opportunities for future deals. Politicians also want to connect to businesses.
>
> For a columnist who writes regularly for a newspaper, business-men give him business clues and news. There are so many people from the financial world. One of my younger class attendants is a deputy manager in Krung Thai Bank.
>
> My class elder with the same running number is an ex-minister. He talked to me and helped all the time. I can ring him any time. This is a new connection I got from attending CMA. I was also invited to give some lessons in CMA later after I graduated. If I had not attended, I would not have had these opportunities. (Interview with an academic member of CMA class 6)

Institutional Networking and the Pursuit of Institutional Interests

Apart from the individual benefits of networking, CMA and TEPCoT clearly use networking to pursue the interests of their parent institutions.

The Stock Exchange of Thailand aims to develop Thailand's capital market to play a significant role in the world financial system. It believes that the main obstacles to this development are the lack of understanding and negative attitudes on the part of individuals and institutions which have a direct or indirect impact on the exchange. The CMA was created as part of a strategy to overcome these two obstacles through two methods: explaining the capital market through the content of the course; and campaigning for policy changes through the network of alumni (interview with an academic member of CMA class 6).

Around half of the course content and activities in the main module of the CMA course is devoted to the importance of developing the Thai capital market. In all, 36 hours out of a total of 60 course hours are devoted to this topic, not including the preliminary course on the basics of the capital market.

The CMA campaigns for policy changes indirectly by explaining its ideas and plans to those who join the course, and directly by presenting proposals to people of political influence, and by seeking support elsewhere in the elite through networking with other executive courses.

On February 27, 2008, the CMA alumni association held a seminar with nine presenters drawn from the first five classes of the CMA, including the head of the Securities and Exchange Commission, the director of the Economic Policy Institute in the Ministry of Finance, a former head of the central bank, and top executives from four leading finance companies. The guests at the seminar included the current minister of finance. The plans, presented as a joint proposal of the five alumni years, were aimed to develop the capital market through "three directions, seven policies, seventeen measures" (*Samakhom nak sueksa* 2008).

After this event, the minister of finance made a proposal to the prime minister to establish a committee for developing the Thai capital market, and the prime minister signed off on the proposal on March 25, 2008.

The committee was established, headed by the minister of finance with the under-secretary of the ministry as his deputy and 23 other members drawn from related government agencies and representatives of the finance industry. Every one of these government agencies had sent members to study at CMA as part of the CMA's policy of targeting institutions which had a bearing on the capital market. All five of the representatives of the finance industry on the committee had studied in CMA's classes 4 and 5. The committee set up subcommittees to draft proposals, and held talks between agencies that had never sat down together in this way before—clearly a result of the CMA's networking. The central bank participated in a subcommittee on proposals for tax incentives for investment. The Ministry of Commerce joined a committee to discuss changes in regulations. The Revenue Department joined a meeting on tax incentives for listed companies to compensate for the costs of their higher accounting standards. The Office of State Enterprise Development joined sessions on overcoming the obstacles to listing subsidiaries of state enterprises on the stock exchange.

The resulting Four-year Plan for Development of the Capital Market (2009–13), which was approved by the committee and presented to the Ministry of Finance, had eight main points (*Ecofocus*, Aug. 10, 2009): end the Stock Exchange of Thailand's monopoly[10] in order to increase efficiency and attract more quality investment and investors into the capital market; have a free market for financial intermediaries, both finance and security companies, in order to increase competition and fairness; reform laws to aid development of the capital market; adjust taxes to incentivize more investment and more trading in stocks; develop new financial products to attract investors; institutionalize the savings system through a national pension fund for informal workers; develop a culture of long-term saving; and develop a secondary bond market.

The key aim of the plan was to liberalize the market, and to move from a structure of mutual-owned or member-owned security companies to investor-owned companies registered on the stock market, in the belief this would broaden the base of stock-holding in the securities sector, increase transparency, and reduce conflict between security companies and other players in the stock market (Atinut and Yanyong 2007). Most of all the reforms aimed to break the hold of a ring of registered securities companies which were able to dictate the policies of the exchange in their own interest and often to the detriment of listed companies and private investors. The Stock Exchange had earlier contracted the Boston Consulting Group to advise on reforms, but their proposals had faced opposition from the securities companies, and been pruned down to some internal reforms, including the launching of CMA. In its first three years, CMA recruited students from among middle-ranking executives in related public and private organizations, concentrated on building good will, and made no moves on policy advocacy. After a new finance minister was appointed in 2008, the CMA developed this plan and presented it to the government. Legislation for demutualization of the stock market was drafted under the Democrat Party-led government (2009–11) and sent for scrutiny by the Council of State (Wilai 2010). After the 2011 election and the return of a Pheu Thai party-led government, the bill was withdrawn.

Disagreement over the legislation focused especially on the fate of a 15-billion baht fund for the development of the capital market, part of which was raised as a levy on the fee income of the member companies in the exchange. Under the reform legislation, the fund would be separated from the exchange and constituted as a non-profit juristic person. The member companies, and the Pheu Thai government, feared that the fund would be misused. The Pheu Thai finance minister also feared that the reforms would transform the stock exchange from a non-profit organization into a business that would fall under the control of a small group of investors, resulting not in greater efficiency but more conflict of interest (Wilai 2010). In other words, in the view of opponents, the stock market reform plan that emerged from the CMA was an ambitious attempt to alter the distribution of interests and benefits from the stock market.

CMA joined with the five other executive courses listed above to create the "six institution network." At the second annual meeting of the network on August 31, 2011, CMA presented its plans for reform of the stock market. The meeting took the form of a discussion with no attempt to reach a conclusion or consensus, yet this presentation marked the beginning of an attempt to build broader support for the proposals through this network, and to create a new platform for building consensus on political and economic issues.

TEPCoT and Policy Networking

The Chamber of Commerce uses the TEPCoT course as a workshop for discussing and formulating policies relating to trade and commerce, and as a channel for introducing these ideas to people in positions of political power and influence. This is evident from the classroom process and the ceremonies of graduation.

The four months of classwork at TEPCoT is organized under three headings: (1) environment analysis (outside-in); (2) national and organization perspective (inside-out); and (3) efficiency strategies and competitiveness. Apart from lectures given as part of the course introduction, all the teaching takes the form of class discussions on pre-determined topics, and the students have to contribute their thoughts to the compilation of a class strategic plan on each of the three topics. At the graduation ceremony for the class, a politically important figure is invited to preside, and part of the event is the presentation of the strategic plans. The ceremony for class 4 was held at the Ministry of Commerce, and the minister of finance presided.

TEPCoT tries to recruit students among people of influence and prominence, and maintains a 50:50 share between the public and private sectors. TEPCoT is also a member of the "six institution net-work," yet has not used its annual meetings to present policy pro-posals relating to trade and commerce. Possibly this is because the members of the Chamber of Commerce are so extremely varied and their interests so diverse that there are few policy issues on which they concur. For this reason, the Chamber of Commerce has not been as forceful and effective a policy advocate as CMA.

Policy Networking and Institutional Interests

The executive courses set up by the Stock Exchange of Thailand and the Thai Chamber of Commerce are mechanisms for achieving certain objectives of the parent organization by recruiting help to devise and promote changes in policy and institutions. Both the CMA and TEPCoT hand-pick students and then encourage them to devise policy plans and help promote these plans among other members of the elite.

The two courses have become highly popular because of the aggregate social, political and economic capital of the students that they recruit or attract. Both the Stock Exchange and the Chamber of Commerce have leveraged the success of these courses to press for policies that they want implemented in the interests of their institu-tion. Rather than education in the true sense, the courses and net-works they have created are a tool to pursue institutional interests within a social framework where decision-making power is distributed across various bodies within a democratic framework. Even so shaping policy is far from easy due to the complexity of the interests involved.

Executive Courses and Billionaire Families

In all, 62 individuals from the families found in *Forbes* maga-zine's list of "Thailand's 40 Richest" for 2011 had attended one or more of the six executive courses. These 62 individuals were drawn from 24 of the 40 families (Table 5.3). The most popular courses were at the National Defense College and the CMA. The attraction of the National Defense College courses probably arose from the large number of senior officials still attending these courses, despite some decline as a result of competition from the new courses. The attraction of the CMA was probably the attendance by prominent politicians. At least one person from almost half of these top lineages

Table 5.3 Executive Course Students on Forbes List of Richest Families, 2011

	National Defense College	Office of Judiciary	KPI	CMA	TEPCoT	Election Commission	Total
Total individuals	34	9	7	32	4	0	62
Total lineages	13	6	6	19	3	0	24

Sources: Calculated from "Thailand's 40 Richest", Brian Mertens, Forbes, 2011, http://www.forbes.com/sites/tatianaserafin/2011/08/30/thailands-40-richest/ and http://www.forbes.com/lists/2011/85/thailand-billionaires-11_rank.html

had attended CMA. By contrast, no single member of these families had attended the course offered by the Election Commission.

The family with the largest number of students was the Chirathiwat family (16), owners of the Central retailing empire, followed by the Shinawatra family in property and telecommunications (8), and the Karnasuta family in construction (7). Two other prominent families, Techaphaibun and Leesawatdikun, that fell outside this top 40 had also contributed many students at these courses.

Although 3 of the top 40 families are in the media business, only 1 individual from these 3 had attended any of these courses, despite the fact that the courses are keen to attract media companies in order to gain publicity.

Conclusion: The Political Economy of Executive Networking

In December 2011, an MP on the parliament's budget scrutiny committee challenged that the award of lucrative contracts by the Meteorological Department had been distorted by the fact that the buyers and sellers had been in the same CMA class. The under-secretary involved had to make a public declaration that, "Everything was done by the book. I do not devote my life to serving friends. We studied together for only a few days. I will not let friendship interfere with principle in carrying out government work" (see *Daily News*, Dec. 12 and 19, 2011). The fact that CMA had invited both the under-secretary and a major contractor of the ministry to the same class raised issues of public concern. Similarly, a telecommunications contract between a state enterprise and a certain business group was investigated by the Counter Corruption Commission after it was exposed that executives from both the state enterprise and the company had attended CMA class 10.

The institutions behind these courses claim that the relations formed among course members and alumni facilitate cooperation between various bodies across the public and private sectors. Yet, as the two examples above illustrate, these courses have been subject to criticism that they provide opportunities for abuse, in particular by fostering relations between those in monitoring roles on the one hand and those they are supposed to be monitoring on the other. According to principles of good governance, there should be some appropriate distance between those who make policy, monitor its impact, and detect offences on the one hand, and those who pursue profit and interest within those policies on the other. It is well known that the motive for enrolling in these courses is not gaining knowledge or pursuing any public benefit but establishing contacts that can be of some personal benefit. As students of CMA reported:

> Although it is not lobbying, we need to keep up connections. If I'm making a TV program and I don't know the right people, how can I sell sponsorships? I sit on the advisory board of Samart Company so I have to follow up things. Whatever occupation one is in, one needs connections.... Everybody says the same: studying in this course is the ultimate. You meet people from every circle for sure.[11]

> I work in politics. When I need information or opinions, I tell my assistant to make an appointment with a businessman to tell me a little about the topic and what the problems are. In the past, I didn't have this kind of connections. But now I have an additional 98 advisors.[12]

> I'm happy to have got close to people in order to exchange inside views. Without regard to each person's official position or whatever, there's openness and a depth of detail which sometimes we cannot find elsewhere. This is an inside track that I like.[13]

These six executive courses have clear objectives of creating networks among their students without any clear indication whether these networks are for public, group or private benefit. Each course attempts to build an image that it is the center of a broad network spanning the elite of administration, politics, economy and society. These networks tend to concentrate power, by creating conditions under which personal relations confer privileges in contravention of principles of good governance whereby the workings of the state should be transparent, fair to all, and subject to checks and balances.

Courses run by state agencies should be subject to regulations that ensure the course are run for private rather than public benefit, that they contribute to the efficiency of the state agency, and that they uphold principles of transparency and good governance. In the case of both the private and public run courses, there should be clear principles governing the enrolment of executives from state agencies based on the benefit to the agency. Several senior executives from state agencies have enrolled in several courses in sequence, at the expense of working time and often in fields unrelated to their official work in any way.

The links of cooperation within the elite created through these courses affect the balance of power in society in several ways. First, they reduce conflict within the elite and lead to a sharing of benefits and privileges under a system of personal cronyism. As a result power over the economy, politics and resources is more concentrated and circumscribed within a small elite. The system of checks and balances is overridden. Outsiders are unable to compete. As a result, the power gap between the elite and the rest gapes wider. Second, these courses serve as a channel to admit new entrants to the elite without generating conflict. In the Thai economy so closely tied to globalization, new economic groups are appearing all the time. The executive courses are a "fast track" for new groups to become part of the elite, by opening the door only just wide enough to admit these new groups, while retaining the structure of barriers that confine the elite within a narrow circle.

Notes

1. This chapter is based on primary research into these quasi-academic institutions. There is no prior literature in Thai or English. The research materials were all in Thai. They included interviews with attendees at these classes, course materials, and publicity by the institutions and alumni groups. Readers who wish to pursue this material are directed to the referencing in the Thai-language version of this article (Nualnoi 2015).

2. Assistant Professor Phramahansa Nithibunyakon, deputy rector for academic affairs, Mahachulalongkorn University.

3. Dr Chingchai Hanchanlash in the TEPCoT course newsletter, issue 1, Oct.–Dec. 2009.

4. Student manual, CMA class 13.
5. "Leader Society, hong rian ni mi tae 'foest klat'" [Leader Society, this classroom for First Class only], Dulyapawin Kronsaeng, *Krungthep Thurakit*, Nov. 24, 2009.
6. Thana Thianachariya, former deputy chairman, TAC group.
7. "Wo to tho, super-connection haeng chon chan nam" [CMA, super-connection for the elite], ASTV online, Dec. 3, 2010, available at http://www.manager.co.th/CelebOnline/ViewNews.aspx?NewsID=9530000170688 [accessed Apr. 8, 2012].
8. "Ko Lo To jap mue ko to mo hai khwam ru kae yaowachon" [Stock exchange joins hands with Bangkok Municipality to provide education for youth], available at http://www.tsi-thailand.org/index.php?option=com_content&task=view&id=1686&Itemid=577 [accessed Apr. 10, 2012].
9. A foundation that supervises several of King Bhumibol's "royal projects." See www.chaipat.or.th.
10. Section 154 of the Securities and Exchange Act 1992 states: "No person other than the Securities Exchange which is established under this Act shall engage in the business of securities exchange or similar business." The English translation of the act is found at http://www.sec.or.th/EN/SECInfo/LawsRegulation/Documents/actandroyal/1Securities.pdf.
11. Raphiphan Luengaramrat, a media lobbyist, reported in *Krungthep Thurakit*, Nov. 24, 2009.
12. Trairong Suwannakhiri, former Democrat Party MP and minister, available at http://www.moneychannel.co.th/Menu6/TradingHour/tabid/86/newsid480/61526/Default.aspx [accessed May 8, 2012].
13. Suwit Khunkitti, former MP and minister, available at http://www.moneychannel.co.th/Menu6/TradingHour/tabid/86/newsid480/61526/Default.aspx [accessed May 8, 2012].

References

Atinut Chaloemphong and Yanyong Thaicharoen. 2007. "Botrian jak kan demutualization talat laksap nai tang prathet" [Learnings from Demutualization in Stock Exchanges Overseas]. Research paper 3/2522. Bangkok: Thai Capital Market Research Institute, Stock Exchange of Thailand.

Embree, J.F. 1950. "Thailand: A Loosely Structured Society." *American Anthropologist* 52: 181–3.

Likhit Dhiravegin. 1978. *The Bureaucratic Elite of Thailand: A Study of Their Sociological Attributes, Educational Backgrounds and Career Advancement Pattern*. Bangkok: Thai Khadi Research Institute.

Nualnoi Treerat. 2015. "Khrueakhai phu borihan sung phan khrueakhai thang kan sueksa phiset" [Executive networks through special courses]. In *Su sangkhom thai samoe na* [*Towards an Equitable Thailand*], ed. Pasuk Phongpaichit. Bangkok: Matichon, pp. 109–47.

Samakhom nak sueksa sathaban withayakan talat thun [CMA Students Association]. 2008. "Raingan kan sammana rueang 'Talat thun thai…khrai ja pha tat" [Thai Capital Market: Who Will Operate?]. Feb., 27.

Unger, Danny. 1998. *Building Social Capital in Thailand: Fibers, Finance, and Infrastructure*. Cambridge: Cambridge University Press.

Wilai Akkharasomchip. 2010. "Kan sueksa kan prae saphap khong talat laksap haeng prathet thai pheua phoem khwam samat nai kan khaeng khan" [Study of Reform of the Stock Exchange of Thailand for Greater Competitiveness]. MA thesis, Political Economy Center, Chulalongkorn University.

6

Network Bureaucracy and Public-Private Firms in Thailand's Energy Sector

Nopanun Wannathepsakul

After the financial crisis of 1997, there emerged in Thailand two major business organizations with a hybrid semi-public, semi-private status. Both are groups of enterprises under a holding company, but each has a different form. PTT Pcl is a state-owned enterprise (SOE), which has been partially privatized as a public company. The Electricity Generating Authority of Thailand (EGAT) is a fully government-owned state enterprise. Both groups have been promoted as "national champions," have grown very fast, and now dominate the petroleum and electricity segments of the energy sector.

In both cases, the holding companies have co-invested with other private or public organizations to create subsidiaries and affiliates. While the holding company holds SOE status and thus is subject to rules and regulations governing SOEs, their subsidiaries may have ambiguous or dual status. Under certain laws, they are treated as a SOE, but under other laws they qualify as a private enterprise and thus have room to do things that a SOE may not. They have been able to expand very fast by exploiting this hybrid and ambiguous status.

Some executives in these organizations are very special. They hold or once held high public office; they are chairpersons or directors on several boards; at the same time they have high positions in public agencies that oversee these organizations. These overlapping functions are allowed by law. Their remuneration from these multiple posts is generous.

These massive hybrid organizations in the energy sector have been created by a "network bureaucracy," which commands great official power. This network spreads across all agencies involved with the energy sector, including the ministries of finance, energy, industry, agriculture, industry, environment, and transport, along with the National Economic and Social Development Board (NESDB), Office of the Attorney General, and other agencies. The hybrid nature of these corporate groups and the power of this "network bureaucracy" have contributed significantly to the rapid expansion of these corporate groups. In one sense this may be seen as a form of "industrial policy" or "catch up industrialization" under which selected companies or sectors are given unusual levels of government assistance in order to develop the scale and capacity needed to be competitive on a world scale. The hybrid nature of these groups allows them to combine the roles of state and entrepreneur in order to overcome problems of risk and coordination. The power of "network bureaucracy" also overcomes problems of coordination.

However, the way in which favors and assistance are conferred on these groups raises many concerns. The selection of these groups for special assistance was not part of any policy subjected to public scrutiny. The multiple roles of certain individuals as policy makers, corporate executives and members of oversight bodies raise questions about conflict of interest, transparency and corporate governance. The exceptional power of "network bureaucracy" can threaten the rights of consumers, the safety of consumers subject to pollution, and the quality of the environment.

This chapter examines the emergence, operation and impact of these new hybrid energy giants, concentrating on PTT, and making reference to EGAT where relevant. It looks especially at PTT's development of projects in the Maptaphut Industrial Estate, and the corporation's reaction to a major campaign to block industrial expansion in the area on grounds of excessive and dangerous pollution.

The first part of this chapter sketches the background to the emergence of these two groups. The second examines the creation of the hybrid public-private firms that now dominate the energy sector. The third introduces "network bureaucracy," the web of linkages between the state agencies and firms involved in the energy sector. The last two sections present case studies of network bureaucracy at work, first in seizing the opportunity presented by the 2006 coup to promote the interests of the leading firms in the sector, and second in countering the most determined attempt yet to impose better controls on industry's impact on health and environment. The conclusion presents a balance sheet of the energy sector's impact on economy and society.

The Emergence of the Energy Giants

The Electricity Generating Authority of Thailand (EGAT) and the Petroleum Authority of Thailand (PTT) were state enterprises created in the early development era (1969 and 1978 respectively). EGAT had a virtual monopoly on electricity generation and transmission. PTT was initially only a major player in oil refining, but after natural gas became the major fuel from the mid-1980s onwards, PTT had a virtual monopoly on management of gas pipelines and a dominant role in gas exploration and petrochemicals. As gas became the principal fuel for electricity generation, the operation of the two firms became closely intertwined.

After the 1997 financial crisis, the IMF demanded that Thailand privatize many state enterprises. A Corporatization Act was passed in 1999 to facilitate the process, and PTT and EGAT headed the list of 59 prospects in a privatization masterplan. PTT was privatized on October 1, 2001 with a sale of around 30 per cent of its shares. The event was controversial because the price was set low, blocks of shares were allocated to political cronies, the remainder sold out in two minutes, and the price subsequently multiplied five times in five years (Bowornwathana and Wescott 2008; Pasuk and Baker 2009: 120–1, and 380n6). Partly as a result, the project to privatize EGAT, in what was planned as the biggest share launch in Thai history, faced opposition from the company union and consumer activist groups. In 2006, the Administrative Court overturned the EGAT privatization, ostensibly on grounds of technical errors in the process, but more generally because of opposition to the sale of public assets and because, as a judge commented, "The court's opinion is that EGAT's privatization benefits only a certain group of people, particularly politicians."[1] The activists attempted to reverse the PTT privatization on similar grounds but the case failed (Pornchai 2012: 64).

Both corporate groups have been heavily promoted by government as "national champions." EGAT has concentrated on defending its near-monopoly of electricity generation and transmission within Thailand, while expanding into similar projects in neighboring countries, especially Laos and Myanmar. Its annual revenues grew from 164 billion baht in 2000 to 536 billion in 2013 (EGAT annual reports).

PTT has been much more expansive. At the time of privatization in 2001, the group already included an upstream exploration arm, PTTEP, interests in four refineries, and four subsidiaries in petrochemicals. By 2013, PTTEP had developed a range of subsidiaries engaged in exploration and production all over the world; the number of petrochemical subsidiaries had grown to nine; two new holding companies oversaw investments in many power companies; and two new subsidiaries oversaw a range of overseas ventures in mining and pipelines. Between 2000 and 2013, PTT's revenues had grown from 371 to 2843 billion baht, net profit from 12 to 95 billion, assets from 230 to 1801 billion, and number of employees from 3,868 to 20,816 (PTT annual reports).[2]

The Hybrid Public-Private Corporation

In Thailand a state-owned enterprise (SOE) is defined as an organization owned by the government or a limited company or partnership in which more than 50 per cent of the share capital is owned by public organizations, state enterprises, or government bodies of various sorts. This definition was laid down in the Budget Procedures Act of 1959.

PTT Pcl is a public company listed on the Stock Exchange of Thailand and also a state enterprise because the Ministry of Finance owns 51 per cent of its share capital. PTT has several subsidiaries, the most important being: PTT Exploration and Production (PTTEP), in which PTT owns 65.29 per cent (as of 31 December 2011); PTT Global Chemical, in which PTT owns 48.92 per cent; and Thai Oil in which PTT owns 49.10 per cent. These subsidiaries have then co-invested with the mother companies in another tier of subsidiaries (see Figure 6.1). For example, PTT Global Chemical and PTT are joint investors in PTT Phenol and PTT Utility. PTT and Thai Oil invested in Thai Oil Power, which in turn invested along with its parent companies in several other subsidiaries including Independent Power Thailand, a company under the Independent Power Producers scheme, and several others under the Small Power Producer scheme.[3] In all of these affiliates, PTT is a minority shareholder but in effect has control. PTT also has two wholly owned subsidiaries, PTT International and PTT Green Energy, which invest in ventures overseas. In all, PTT counts 46 companies as part of the "PTT group."

EGAT, which is a SOE wholly owned by the Ministry of Finance, has two subsidiaries: EGCO in which EGAT holds 25.41 per cent, and Ratchaburi Holdings in which EGAT holds 45 per cent. EGCO in turn holds an 18.72 per cent stake in East Water, while Ratchaburi has several co-investments with other companies in electricity producers such as Ratchaburi Power and Nava Nakorn Electricity Generating. Apart from EGAT, all these companies qualify as private enterprises.

All the PTT subsidiaries and affiliates have the status as private enterprises under certain laws. As a private enterprise, they may receive promotional privileges from the Board of Investment, and are not bound by regulations imposed on SOEs by the Ministry of Finance and other government agencies. Yet through their association with PTT, these subsidiaries can claim some of the advantages of being an SOE. For example, the Ministry of Finance can guarantee their loans, the Office of the Attorney General will mount the defense if they are brought to court, and the Council of State may offer advice in any legal dispute.

The ambiguous status of these companies has arisen because there are many laws on state enterprises, and the definitions in these laws are not the same. A company may qualify as a state enterprise according to one law and as a private enterprise under another law (Phairot et al. 2009).

For example, PTTEP is a state enterprise under the Budget Procedures Act 1959 because a state enterprise holds more than 50 per cent of its share capital. As such, under the Petroleum Act 1971 it may hold concessions for exploration of petroleum without getting approval of the cabinet, yet at the same time enjoy privileges of a state enterprise, such as gaining state support to enter into joint ventures overseas that the government treats as government-to-government collaboration.

The Act on Qualification Standards for Directors of State Enterprises 1975 requires a subsidiary to have a two-thirds government share ownership to qualify as an SOE. Hence under this Act, PTTEP and several other PTT subsidiaries are classed as private enterprises.

PTT Green Energy is a SOE which has support of the Energy Ministry to develop alternative energy sources, including overseas investments in palm oil. Another subsidiary, Combined Heat and Power

Production, is treated as a SOE and has sole rights to supply electricity to a major government office complex in Bangkok, but also has Board of Investment privileges waiving corporate tax and import duty on machinery.

As a result, the status of these semi-public semi-private organizations may be subject to legal interpretation, which is determined by government lawyers (usually the Office of the Council of State) and thus biased towards the government's benefit.

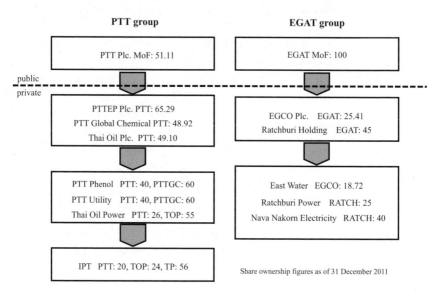

Figure 6.1 PTT and EGAT as Semi-Public Semi-Private Organizations

Network Bureaucracy in the Energy Sector

Officials in certain ministries and public offices now have power to control and direct these large semi-public semi-private companies in the energy sector. They have the authority to make regulations, issue licenses and grant permissions. These powers come from their ex officio authority as officials, as stipulated by laws.

The Energy Ministry is at the center of Thailand's energy policy. Officials in this ministry hold positions in many important boards and committees relating to the energy sector (Figure 6.2). The important ones are the National Energy Policy Council (NEPC), the Energy Policy Management Committee (EPMC), and the Power Development Plan Committee (PDPC).

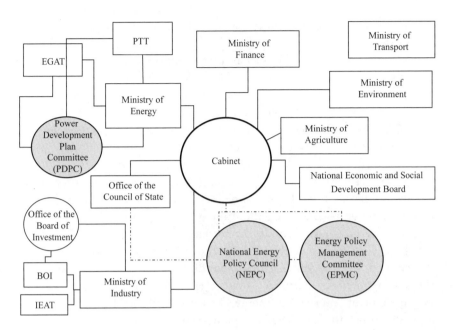

Figure 6.2 The Structure of Authority in the Energy Sector

All three of these bodies are chaired by the same person, the under-secretary of Ministry of Energy. Other members are high-ranking officials, including: the director-generals and under-secretaries of the industry, environment, finance, agriculture, and transport ministries; the secretary-generals of the NESDB and the Office of the Council of State; the director-general of the Energy Policy and Planning Office (EPPO), the governor of EGAT, and the managing director of PTT. The coordinators of the network are the under-secretary of energy and the director of EPPO.

At the national level, the National Energy Policy Council (NEPC) draws up an energy plan, for approval by the cabinet. The implementation and administration rest with the energy minister, his under-secretary, and the director-generals of key departments through some key coordinating committees.

The Energy Policy Management Committee (EPMC) controls the oil fund (a revolving fund used to adjust prices of different fuels by levies and subsidies), and has the power to set the rates for levies and subsidies on various fuels. The minister of energy officially chairs the Committee but sometimes delegates the chair to the under-secretary of energy. The under-secretaries of several other relevant ministries are committee members.

At the next level of policy implementation, administered by the under-secretary of the Ministry of Energy, there are several key committees. The Petroleum Committee advises cabinet on granting concessions for petroleum exploration, and on the level of royalties. The Fuel Oil Control Committee has the authority to grant concessions for fuel storage facilities or the transportation of petroleum by pipelines. The Power Development Plan Committee determines future energy investment projects. These and other offices and boards on energy policy all include the under-secretary of the Energy Ministry and the director-general of the Energy Policy and Planning Office, and the key ones also include the secretary-general of the NESDB.

In theory policy is decided by the cabinet. In practice policy is determined by key officials in a handful of departments, especially the Department of Mineral Fuels, Department of Energy Business, Department of Alternative Energy Development and the Energy Policy and Planning Office. The companies under the care of all these government departments are the PTT and EGAT groups.

The Rewards of Network Bureaucracy

For the officials and executives involved in network bureaucracy in the energy sector, the rewards are significant. For example in 2009, the meeting allowances and average bonus for a director of PTT Chemical was 2.75 million baht; for PTT, 2.67 million; Thai Oil, 2.63 million; PTTEP, 2.48 million; IRPC, 1.43 million; EGCO, 1.62 million; and Ratchaburi Holding, 1.15 million.

Those at the top of the tree of network bureaucracy benefit from multiple directorships. For example, the under-secretary of the Energy Ministry in 2006 was a director or chairperson of seven organizations (PTT, NPT, Rayong Refinery, PTT Chemical, PTTEP, Ratchaburi Electricity Plant and Thai Oil) and took home allowances and bonuses of 8 million baht. The successor in the post in 2008 was chairperson or director in three organizations (PTT Chemical, PTT Aromatics, EGCO) and took home 7.3 million baht. The next successor in 2009 was chairperson in three organizations (PTT, PTT Aromatics, IRPC) and took home 5.4 million baht.

These semi-public private companies are a source of benefit for several groups, particularly officials in the network. As officials gain official promotion, they also move up the scale of companies, from those where the remuneration is low to those where it is better. Posts are circulated within the network, and at official retirement are passed down to successors in office (Senate Committee on Corruption 2010a).

Network Bureaucracy and Conflicts of Interest

In order to prevent conflicts between private interest and public interest, the Counter-Corruption Commission Act 1999 prohibits government officials from sitting on the boards of directors of private companies that hold concession contracts, or engage in joint investments with a government agency that the official oversees. Yet within the tangled structure of the energy bureaucracy, this stipulation is ignored.

Under the existing structure and regulations, it is difficult to separate the roles of policy-making, oversight and management. Some officials act as policy-makers and overseers for companies in which they have a management role.

For example, the under-secretary of the Ministry of Energy is an ex officio member of all the key policy bodies described above (NEPC, PDPC, EPMC). At the same time, this official also chairs the board of PTT and some of its subsidiaries.

The Energy Ministry and EPPO oversee PTT. At certain periods the under-secretary of the Energy Ministry has been chairman of the Petroleum Committee, chairman of the Fuel Oil Control Committee, a member of NEPC, member of PDPC, and also chairman of the board of PTT, chairman of PTT Aromatics, chairman of PTT Chemical (now PTT Global Chemical) and chairman of EGAT.

Similarly, the director-general of EPPO is an ex officio member of several of the committees overseeing policy making and implementation, such as the Petroleum Committee and EPMC. At the same time, this official sits on the board of PTTEP.

These duplications give rise to conflict of interest but are not against the law. Two cases illustrate the complications that can arise.

Between 2006 and 2010, the under-secretary of the Energy Ministry was both an ex officio member of EPMC and the chairperson of PTT. Between 2007 and 2011, as part of a policy to promote alternative energy sources, the government repeatedly reduced the Oil Fund levy, while raising the rate of subsidy for the production of gasohol. On April 20, 2007, the PTT board resolved to establish

PTT Green Energy in Singapore, with PTT holding 100 per cent ownership. The major purpose of the new company was to invest in oil palm production to produce gasohol (Fact Sheet, PTT Pcl 2012: 143). In December 2011, the subsidy rates were 2.80 baht per liter for gasohol E20, and 13.50 baht per liter for gasohol E85. These payments amounted to subsidies for the oil palm project.

In principle, subsidizing the promotion of investment in alternative energy is a reasonable policy. If small private producers had access to the subsidy, the policy would also promote competition in the energy sector. But PTT is a large corporation whose main product is not alternative energy. Subsidizing such a company does not improve competition in the energy industry. In effect, the Oil Fund was used to subsidize the cost of production of a subsidiary of PTT.

Combined Heat and Power Production was established as a fully owned subsidiary of PTT. It supplies coolant and electricity to government offices via Dhanarak Asset Development, a company owned by the Treasury Department under the Ministry of Finance (Fact Sheet, PTT Pcl 2012: 77–8). It also sells electricity to the Metropolitan Electricity Authority. At the time Combined Heat and Power Production was established, one of PTT's directors was an official of the Treasury Department and became its director-general in the following year. She was also a director of Dhanarak Asset Development and of the Metropolitan Electricity Authority.

Combined Heat and Power Production is a SOE partly owned by the Ministry of Finance (via its investment in PTT). Several of its directors are government officials. Some, including those who represent PTT on the board, also sit on the committees overseeing the industry. Some are from the Office of the Attorney General, which acts as legal advisor to the public sector. As a public enterprise, Combined Heat and Power Production was given an exclusive right to sell power from EGAT to government offices, and was allowed to rent land from the Treasury Department for its plant. At the same time, the company also qualified to receive promotional privileges from the Board of Investment (import tax exemptions on imported machinery, and a 8-year holiday for corporate income tax). Furthermore, the company was treated as a state enterprise under the new Private Investment in State Undertakings Act 2013 and thus exempted from various strict regulations governing a private enterprise working with a government agency such as having a bidding procedure to select a construction contractor, having the Office of the Attorney General scrutinize its contracts, or needing cabinet approval for any investment project.

When government officials simultaneously play roles as officials overseeing the company and as directors looking after the interest of the company, the interests of the corporation and the public interests overlap and could be in conflict. The result also may be to create a non-level playing field in which certain types of enterprises have the best of both worlds as both a private enterprise and a public one.

The Energy Industry after the 2006 Coup

After the coup on September 19, 2006, the 1997 constitution was suspended and a new charter drafted by an appointed national assembly comprised mostly of retired bureaucrats and generals, with some technocrats and academics. The cabinet in power for over a year before the next election was headed by a general and comprised mostly of retired officials and technocrats. In this period, when bureaucrats had the dominant role in politics, several laws relating to the energy industry were amended or introduced to benefit the semi-public semi-private companies, especially those in the electricity and petroleum sectors. Three cases will be discussed here.

Amendment of the Petroleum Act in 2007

According to the Petroleum Act 1971, the Petroleum Committee makes recommendations to the cabinet concerning the exploration and production of petroleum. The committee has power to grant or extend concessions for exploration or production of petroleum, transfer a concession, and adjust the rates of royalties levied on concessionaires. The committee also has the authority to set the well-head price of natural gas through negotiation with the concessionaire. Under the Act, each company was limited to a maximum of five concession areas for exploration and production, not exceeding a total of 20,000 square kilometers. Several companies, including PTTEP, got round this limit by establishing subsidiaries, but this device was clumsy and difficult.

An amendment to the Petroleum Act was passed by the coup government in 2007. This amendment transferred the power to grant, amend or transfer concessions for the exploration of petroleum from the cabinet to the minister of energy. It also removed the stipulation in the 1971 act limiting any concession to five sites not exceeding a total of 20,000 square kilometers. Under the original act, the rate of royalties was decided by the cabinet, and the maximum discount allowed at the discretion of the Petroleum Committee was 30 per cent. Under the 2007 amendment, the authority for determining the rate of royalties was transferred to the minister of energy, and the maximum discount raised to 90 per cent.

In the 42 days between the passage of this amendment and the expiry of the coup government, 22 concessions for oil exploration were granted to private companies, for a total of 27 areas, 8 in the gulf and 19 on land (Senate Committee on Corruption 2010b).

A few days after the 2007 amendment, the cabinet approved a proposal by the Energy Ministry to give 10-year extensions to the exploration concessions of two consortia, one headed by Chevron Thai and the other by PTTEP. The cabinet also instructed the Energy Ministry to grant four new concessions on petroleum exploration, three of which involved PTTEP in conjunction with its own subsidiaries and other private companies including Chevron Thai.

In sum, the 2007 amendment to the Petroleum Act removed the limit on concession areas and increased the discretion of the minister and director-general of the Energy Ministry in administering the concessions. Immediately after this amendment, many new concessions were given, and many old ones extended, to the benefit of companies in the PTT group.

Amendments to the Standard Qualifications for Directors and Employees of State-owned Enterprises 2007

The Counter-Corruption Commission Act 1999 prohibits government officials from sitting on the boards of directors of private companies that hold concession contracts or engage in joint investments with a government agency that the official oversees.

PTTEP has been granted concessions for exploration and production of oil under the oversight of the Ministry of Energy. Hence, according to the Counter Corruption Commission Act of 1999, no official from the Ministry of Energy may sit on its board. However, under the coup government in 2007, the Act on the Standard Qualifications for Directors and Employees of State-owned Enterprises was amended to allow high-level government officials to sit on the boards of companies which receive concessions from government and in which state enterprises have a stake. After this amendment, the director-general of the Department of Mineral Resources became chairman of PTTEP, replaced in 2012 by the under-secretary of the Ministry of Energy who was also simultaneously chairman of PTT. At exactly this time, the PTTEP also had its concession extended (as described above) under the conditions created by the amendment of the Petroleum Act.

The Energy Act 2007 and the Natural Gas Pipelines Masterplan, 2001–11

The year 2007 was a critical period for the energy sector. PTT's privatization was being challenged in the courts. The Energy Act 2007 was passed with a stated aim to ensure good governance, consumer protection, efficiency and fair competition in the energy sector, in order to counter criticism that the partial privatization of the energy sector had resulted in rent-seeking, conflict of interest and lack of regulation. However, in the few months immediately before the court decision on PTT and before the Energy Act came into force on December 10, 2007, the cabinet made several key decisions relating to the energy sector. It approved PTT's plan for a natural gas pipeline system. Following this, NEPC approved new rates for gas transmission and assigned the Energy Policy and Planning Office (EPPO) to prepare a manual for determining gas prices and gas transmission charges. The manual was prepared and approved in the period when officials were in command of energy policy.

Gas transmission at this time was a pure monopoly of PTT, not open to third parties. Gas transmission is a business in which the initial investment costs are high but the subsequent operating costs are low. In such situations, once a first mover has made the investment, potential competitors are shut out. The approval of the masterplan and the preparation of a manual for calculating gas transmission charges were completed before the court decision on the rollback of the PTT privatization and before a new regime of monitoring was introduced under the Energy Act. Approving PTT's investment plan worth 160 billion baht effectively confirmed PTT's monopoly in the future, while the new manual allowed PTT to raise the gas transmission charge, resulting in a hike in electricity charges, since EGAT calculates the charge by a cost-plus formula. This formula cannot be changed by the Energy Regulatory Commission established under the Energy Act.

The aim of the Energy Act 2007 was to separate policy-making, monitoring, and operation of energy businesses; to create opportunities for private enterprise, communities and citizens to have larger roles; and to increase efficiency and ensure fair pricing.

The act created an Energy Regulatory Commission but failed to define its authority. It oversees the pricing of gas and electricity but has no authority over the well-head price of gas, leaving that governed by other legislation (Praipol and Puree 2008; Duenden 2013). Despite these failings, the passage of the act nominally separated monitoring and operation of energy businesses. This resolved one of the issues raised in the case to have the privatization of PTT overturned.

In late 2007, the Administrative Court ruled that PTT should return public assets to the state. Following this ruling, the gas pipelines were returned to state ownership, but the right to use those assets remained with PTT under the existing monopoly arrangement. So in effect PTT retained its monopoly on gas transmission and its investments in gas pipelines. The objective of separating state and private interests was not achieved (Duenden 2013).

In sum, after the 2006 coup, there were several changes in energy policy, namely reducing the government royalties on petroleum, approving the masterplan for gas pipelines, setting the formula for gas pricing, passing the Energy Act, and passing an amendment allowing officials to remain directors in private companies holding government concessions. This flurry of laws and rules strengthened both PTT and the network bureaucracy in the energy sector.

Network Bureaucracy and Pollution at Maptaphut

Maptaphut, situated on the Eastern Seaboard in Rayong Province, is the largest industrial estate in Thailand. It came into being after the discovery of gas deposits in the Gulf of Thailand in the early 1980s. Promotion of the energy industry and related heavy industries became part of Thailand's strategy of industrialization. To permit the construction of petrochemical factories which process raw materials derived from oil refineries and natural gas separation plants, clauses prohibiting petrochemical industries were deleted from the plan of Rayong Province where the estate is situated. The original area of 8,000 rai (1,280 ha) was expanded to six times that area in 2003.

By 2007, five industrial zones at Maptaphut were generating 558,000 tons of waste a year, of which 31 per cent was hazardous.

Environmental activists raised concern over the resulting pollution and the health impact on local communities, but were unable to limit the expansion of the estate. In April 2007 a petition was sent to the National Environmental Board (NEB) to declare Maptaphut a pollution control zone according to the Environment Act 1992, but the NEB rejected the petition for fear of the impact on investment (Bamphen and Somphon 2008: 152).

On October 1, 2007, a group of residents from 11 communities in the industrial zone filed a complaint with the Rayong Administrative Court charging the NEB with negligence for failing to declare Maptaphut a pollution control zone as required by law. On March 3, 2009, the Court ruled in the communities' favor, and ordered the NEB to declare all areas in and around Maptaphut a pollution control zone within 60 days. The NEB complied with the order and created the zone, but also launched an appeal against the court ruling.

This court victory had implications for new investment projects which were now required to include a plan to protect the health of local communities from industrial pollution and to undergo a health impact assessment before the project could proceed.

PTT was one of the companies affected. In 2007 the cabinet had approved PTT's long-term plan for natural gas supply which included 14 investment projects, totaling over 150 billion baht, in gas pipelines, a gas separation plant and an electricity generation plant. PTT had also launched several new projects in joint venture with the Siam Cement Group. Several of these projects were located in the Maptaphut industrial estate.

Business groups argued that the court ruling was harmful to investment and economic growth. They claimed that the pollution problem was not critical as the majority of the companies in the estate had adequate standards of pollution control. They pointed out that Maptaphut contributed 11 per cent of Thailand's GDP and employed over 100,000 workers. They suggested the economy would suffer as potential investors would relocate elsewhere (Bangkok Post 2010). Despite the declaration of the zone, many of the expansion projects were not halted.

On June 19, 2009, the Stop Global Warming Association, an NGO headed by a legal activist, Srisuwan Janya, filed a complaint with the Administrative Court against eight government agencies for illegally allowing expansion of plants in the estate to continue. On September 29, 2009 the court ruled that 76 projects must be temporarily stopped because they had failed to undergo the health impact assessment required under Article 67 of the constitution.[4]

Network Bureaucracy and the Maptaphut Issue

The estimated value of the 76 projects was 400 billion baht (around US$10 billion). Business associations, leaders of the energy industry, and the Japanese government expressed horror at the impact of these suspensions on the economy and on the future of Thailand's industrialization (Bangkok Pundit 2010). The National Environment Board launched an appeal against the court ruling. The government contemplated making a quick amendment of the Environment Act, but backed down for fear of provoking more opposition from civil society. Instead, in November 2009 it appointed a committee, headed by former prime minister Anand Panyarachun, tasked to create a mechanism for overcoming the problems at Maptaphut.

Network bureaucracy sprang into action to guide this process. Major corporate groups including PTT and EGAT gave opinions to the Anand Committee on the technical issues. The Ministry of Industry, Industrial Estate Authority of Thailand, and Energy Regulatory Commission sent letters to the Office of the Council of State to ask advice on legal matters.

The Council of State assigned two expert committees to discuss the issue. These included five people who were directors in PTT-related companies.[5] The Office of the Council of State gave advice that, as an independent organization for assessing the environment and health impact of projects had not been established, the existing law should be followed, namely the Environment Act of 1992. The two committees concluded in summary that, since there was no independent body to draft a law setting guidelines for defining projects of potentially severe impact on communities, the existing law should be used, namely section 67 of the 2007 constitution (see note 4). This section allowed relevant agencies to grant permission to a project as long as there had been a health and environment impact assessment, and a public hearing by stakeholders.[6]

This ruling in effect declared that the bureaucratic agencies had the authority to allow the suspended projects to go ahead, but would need to show that the environmental and health impacts of the projects had been assessed. Following this ruling, the Ministry of Environment made an announcement on the rules, methods, regulations and directions for health impact assessments. The Office of Environmental Policy and Planning evaluated reports on the impact of the new projects. In June 2010, the Anand Committee announced a list of 18 categories of projects that should be considered "harmful activities" requiring full health and environmental assessments. The Anand Committee also established a temporary mechanism for undertaking and evaluating health and environmental assessments. The National Environment Board (NEB) considered the Anand Committee's list, and reduced the number of categories classified as "harmful activities" from 18 to 11. The cabinet rapidly approved the NEB's decision. Before the NEB dropped the "harmful" activities to 11 types, there were 57 projects still suspended, some belonging to PTT. But after the NEB took action, the court ruled in September 2010 that only two of the 57 projects fell within the Ministry of Industry's list of "harmful activities," and allowed the other 55 to proceed. Thus eventually only 2 of the 76 suspended projects were disallowed.[7]

Two things were crucial to the result of this process. The first was the Council of State's decision that it would be legal to find a way around the constitutional provision (as achieved through the Anand Committee). The second was the listing of categories of "harmful activities." Environmental activists and the big power companies offered very different technical advice on these issues. Two examples will suffice.

In the case of petrochemical plants, the environmentalists argued that new projects above a certain capacity (different depending on the process) should be required to undergo assessment, along with all expansion projects that increased the capacity by 35 per cent or more. The committee accepted this recommendation. NEB retained the capacity ceilings for new projects, but removed the requirement for any expansion project above 35 per cent. With this adjustment, all but one of the petrochemical expansion projects escaped the need for assessment, including two projects of PTT Asahi Chemical and one of PTT Phenol.

In the case of power generation, EGAT representatives argued that gas-powered plants should be excluded as their pollution was minimal, and that ceiling limits for coal-powered and combined-cycle power plants should be set quite high as EGAT now used better technology than in the past (EGAT 2010; Subcommittee on Public

Hearing 2010). Environmentalists argued that all large plants had risks of air and water pollution and thus should be subject to assessment (National Environment Board 2010). The committee thus proposed a 700 MW ceiling for gas-powered plants and a 1,000 MW ceiling for combined cycle plants. The NEB adjusted these limits upwards, setting 3000 MW as the ceiling for combined cycle or co-generation plants, and placing no limit for gas. This closely followed EGAT's proposal.

The Anand Committee expressed dismay at the NEB's adjustment of its list. The environmental lobby was devastated that this campaign had failed to halt a massive expansion at a site where pollution problems were already severe, and that the event had set a precedent for eluding health and environmental assessments.[8] PTT's net profit increased steadily from 65.5 billion baht in 2009 to 84.0 billion in 2010 and 106.2 billion in 2011.

In the Maptaphut case, a small number of officials were able to define what constituted a "severe risk to health." As a result, many others suffered a decline in the quality of their lives, and a further loss of faith in the agencies of the state. The outcome of the Maptaphut dispute was a tragedy for communities, health and environment. The roots of this tragedy lie in the monopolies of economic and political power which stand in opposition to principles of democracy, human rights, equity, participation and transparency.

Conclusion

In one sense, the political support for these energy companies has generated rapid growth and created "national champions" that can compete at international level. A similar policy was followed by European countries after World War Two and later by Japan and the Asian NICs.[9]

However, in these above cases, the promotion of "national champions" was based on explicit policy, subject to public debate, and generally bound by certain principles and rules. The promotion of "national champions" in the energy sector in present-day Thailand, by contrast, is not based on any explicit policy and is achieved largely by subverting rules and principles that are applied to others.

Semi-public semi-private companies have been created to facilitate rapid growth in the energy sector. PTT makes a large annual profit from petroleum and petroleum-related industries, especially from oil, natural gas and petrochemical products. It is a public company, listed on the Stock Exchange of Thailand. Yet it receives all kinds of privileges and benefits from the government. As a state enterprise, PTT's many privileges include an exclusive right to explore and produce petroleum products, a monopoly on the sale of petroleum to government offices, loans guaranteed by the Ministry of Finance, and legal assistance from the Office of the Attorney General. Most important of all, it has privileged access to policy making and implementation through network bureaucracy. Yet at the same time, PTT has invested in a range of subsidiaries which have the status of private enterprises. As such, they qualify for investment privileges from the Board of Investment, and evade restrictions placed on SOEs by the Ministry of Finance and other agencies.

In yet another twist of favoritism, some of these companies have further privileges. PTTEP is allowed exception from the counter-corruption law forbidding officials to be executives in concession companies, and is allowed exception from the 2013 law on public-private joint ventures.

The public gain from these arrangements in terms of the energy sector's contribution to economic growth is undeniably significant. The private gain to the individuals involved in the energy sector's network bureaucracy is also impressive. But these gains are more than balanced by losses elsewhere.

The advantages given to these favored firms tilt the playing field in their favor to the detriment of other firms. PTT Green Energy receives semi-disguised subsidies for production of gasohol which gives them advantages over competitors. Combined Heat and Power Production not only has the privilege of being a 100 per cent owned SOE yet being granted investment privileges as a private company, but also has the extra advantage of sharing directors with the agencies that are its main customers.

The multiple roles of officials as makers of policy, directors and executives of firms operating under those policies, and members of oversight bodies supervising policy implementation creates risks for good governance because of conflicts between private and public interest. This situation has given rise to concerns among consumers that there may not be fair pricing in the energy sector.[10]

In particular, EGAT has a near monopoly on electricity generation and PTT has a monopoly on the distribution of natural gas. Government policy towards industry claims to favor competition as a means to achieve efficiency, yet in practice the government has helped to strengthen and defend these monopolies. Since the 2007 Energy Act, the Energy Regulatory Commission has been created to provide better public oversight of this sector. But the remit of the Commission seems to have been deliberately limited in order to reduce its effectiveness, and efforts were made to protect and prolong PTT's privileged position before this new oversight regime came into force. As EGAT has a monopoly on electricity generation and makes better profits the more it sells, there is no incentive to seriously economize on electricity usage or to seek alternative forms of energy.

The state is not interested in promoting greater competition because monopolies deliver high profits, most of which accrues to the government. But not all. Forty-nine per cent of PTT is privately owned. As a result, almost half of the immense profits of its privileged operations goes into the pockets of a few thousand shareholders, many of whom hold those shares through political connections.[11]

The privileged position of these companies poses threats to citizens as consumers and to the environment. The problems of pollution at Maptaphut have been known for over two decades. Many reports have shown that the problem has grown steadily worse, while countless protests and petitions have delivered no result. In 2007–08, civil society groups tried to mobilize the Environment Law, the 2007 constitution, and the new structure of administrative courts to halt the trend. The initial decision, halting the implementation of 76 projects, was instantly hailed as a landmark in the history of Thailand's environmentalism. Yet within two years, the court ruling had been effectively nullified. The attempt to establish the principles for better safeguarding of health and environment in industrial planning had resulted in the exact opposite—a precedent for how to evade such principles. This reversal was achieved by mobilizing the power of the energy sector's network bureaucracy.

This case, in which protected monopolies deliver high benefits to a few while having severe implications on the health and well-being of hundreds of thousands of people, is a powerful example of inequality in Thailand today.

Notes

1.   Supreme Administrative Court on Black Case No For 14/2548 and Red Case No For 5/2549. See further information on Thai Supreme Court at http://www.admincourt.go.th/amc_eng.aspx.

2. See Moody's evaluation of PTT on Apr. 10, 2013, at http://ptt.listed company.com/misc/CR/20130510-PTT-Moody-EN.pdf [accessed Feb. 7, 2014].

3. EGAT has a monopoly right to sell electricity, but other companies may generate power and sell to EGAT under the Small Power Producer and Independent Power Producer schemes initiated in 1992 and 1994 respectively.

4. Article 67 of the 2007 constitution reads: "Any project or activity which may seriously affect the quality of the environment, natural resources and biological diversity shall not be permitted, unless its impacts on the quality of the environment and on health of the people in the communities have been studied and evaluated and consultation with the public and interested parties have been organised, and opinions of an independent organisation, consisting of representatives from private environmental and health organisations and from higher education institutions providing studies in the field of environment, natural resources or health, have been obtained prior to the operation of such project or activity.

    The right of a community to sue a government agency, State agency, State enterprise, local government organisation or other State authority which is a juristic person to perform the duties under this section shall be protected."

5. Aree Wongareeya, director of IRPC; Manu Liaophairat, director of PTT Chemical, PTTEP, Thai Oil and Thai Oil Power; Chirdpong Siriwit, director of PTT, PTT Chemical, PTT Aromatic, Thai Oil, IRPC, National Petroleum, Rayong Refinery, PTTEP, Ratchaburi Electricity Production; Chakramon Pasukwanit, director of PTT, Thai Oil, Indorama Venture; and Wisut Srisuphan, director of PTTEP.

6. Council of State ruling 491-493/2552 dated July 30, 2009.

7. One of the two was an ethylene project by a PTT subsidiary, TOC Glycol. However, PTT was generally happy with the ruling as the release of other projects meant its gas separation plant would be able to go ahead. See http://www.bloomberg.com/news/2010-09-02/thai-court-lifts-ban-on-industrial-projects-halted-on-environment-grounds.html.

8. See for example, "Map Ta Phut: Thailand's Minamata?", *Focus* 68 (June 2012), at http://www.hurights.or.jp/archives/focus/section2/2012/06/map-ta-phut-thailands-minamata.html.

9. For a comprehensive survey of this strategy, from 19th-century Europe, through the post-Second World War era, to Japan and the Asian NICs, see Suehiro (2008).

10. Since the mid-2000s, a group of consumer-protection groups, spearheaded by Rossana Tositrakul, a former senator, has repeatedly challenged PTT over monopolistic practices. The group claims that PTT exploits monopolies provided under current laws to overcharge consumers

for the benefit of its shareholders. After the 2014 coup, the group also challenged PTT's management of concessions for exploration for petrol and gas.

11. The initial sale of shares in PTT in 2001 resulted in several politicians connected to the government of the time becoming large shareholders. See Pasuk and Baker 2009: 120–1 and 380n6.

References

Annual reports of PTT and EGAT. Available at http://www.pttplc.com/en/ Media-Center/Pages/Annual-Report.aspx and http://www.egat.co.th/en/ index.php?option=com_content&view=article&id=165&Itemid=146.

Bamphen Chairak and Somphon Phengkam, ed. 2008. *Anakhot rayong sen thang su sangkhom sukaphap* [The Future of Rayong: Route to a Healthy Society]. Bangkok: National Health Commission Office.

Bangkok Post. 2010. "Japanese Warn of Dire Outcome Again," Jan. 29. Available at www.bdo-thaitax.com/bdo/in-the-news/79.

Bangkok Pundit. 2010. "Checking in on the Map Ta Phut Impasse." July 19. At http://asiancorrespondent.com/37690/checking-in-on-the-map-ta-phut-industrial-estate-impasse-2/.

Bowornwathana, Bidhya and Clay Wescott, ed. *Comparative Governance Reform in Asia: Democracy, Corruption, and Government Trust.* Bingley, WA: Emerald Group.

Duenden Nikomborirak. 2013. "Gas in Thailand, Priorities and Pathways in Services Reform. Part II." *World Scientific Studies in International Economics* 25: 45–65.

EGAT. 2010. "Ekkasan prakop kan chi jaeng khrongkan rong fai fa kas thammachat mai pen khrongkan ruea kitakam thi at ko hai koet phon krathop runraeng to chumchon tam ratthamanun pho so 2550 matra 67 wak song" [Documents explaining that the natural-gas electricity generating plant is not a project or activity that will cause severe impact to communities according to the 2007 constitution clause 67(2)]. Available at http://www.publicconsultation.opm.go.th/rubfung67/doc84.pdf.

Fact Sheet, PTT Pcl 2012. "Baep sadaeng raikan khomun lae nangsue chichuan. Sup khomun samkhan khong tra san (Fact Sheet) phuea ok hun ku mai mi prakan khong borisut khrang thi 2/2555 khrop kamnot thai thon pi pho so 2562" [Reporting form, summary of important data (fact sheet) for issue of the company's unsecured shares, number 2/2013 for redemption in 2019].

National Environment Board. 2010. *Ekkasan prakob kan prachum khana kammakan sing waetlom haeng chat* [Documents for meeting of NEB]. Meeting 4/2010, document 1.

Pasuk Phongpaichit and Chris Baker. *Thaksin*. 2nd edition. Chiang Mai: Silkworm Books, 2009.

Phairot Wongwipanon et al. 2009. *Thammaphiban nai ongkon rat: korani sueksa rat wisahakit thai* [Good Governance in State Agencies: Case Study of Thai State Enterprises]. Bangkok: Thailand Research Fund.

Pornchai Wisuttisak. 2012. "Liberalization of the Thai Energy Sector: A Consideration of Competition Law and Sectoral Regulation." *Journal of World Energy Law and Business* 5, 1: 60–77.

Praipol Koomsup and Puree Sirasoontorn. 2008. *Energy Act: Implications for the Energy Sector in Thailand*. Discussion Paper No. 0013. September 15. Faculty of Economics, Thammasat University.

Senate Committee on Corruption. 2010a. *Raingan kan phicharana sueksa rueang thammaphiban nai rabop phalang ngan khong prathet* [Report on Good Governance in the Country's Energy Sector]. Prepared for Senate meeting 26, May 4.

————. 2010b. *Raingan kan phicharana sueksa rueang thammaphiban nai rabop phalang ngan khong prathet* [Report on Good Governance in the Country's Energy Sector], part 2, May 2009–December 2010.

Subcommittee on Public Hearing. 2010. *Khrongkan ruea kitakan thi at ko hai koet phon kathop to chumchon yang run raeng dan thang khunaphap sing waetlom sapyakon thammachat lae sukhaphap jamnuan 18 praphet* [List of 18 projects and activities that may have severe impact on the quality of environment, natural resources, and health of communities]. Presented to the prime minister, June 21.

Suehiro, Akira. 2008. *Catch-up Industrialization: The Trajectory and Prospects of East Asian Economies*. Singapore: NUS Press, 2008.

7

Inequalities of Local Power and Profit: The Changing Structure of Provincial Power

Chaiyon Praditsil and Chainarong Khrueanuan[1]

Analysis of inequality in Thailand often highlights the gap in income, wealth, and power between the capital on the one hand and the provinces on the other. While this gap is certainly significant, concentrating on this aspect alone is misleading. In the provinces also, inequality may be high. In 2009, for instance, the Gini Index for the Central Region was 0.45, same as the nationwide figure. Within 14 of the 73 provinces nationwide, the Gini was higher than 0.5 (NSO Poverty Map 2009, reported in UNDP 2014: 148–9).

In the period up to the 1960s, both political power and economic development were highly concentrated in the capital city of Bangkok. From the 1970s, this changed to some extent. With diversification in agriculture, investments in infrastructure (especially electricity and roads), and policies to relocate industry away from the capital, provincial economies became more buoyant. With parliament becoming more established, and later with decentralization to local government, power was to some extent redistributed away from the center. Across Thailand, local politics became more dynamic. And across Thailand in many provinces, there emerged a family or small groups of families that dominated both the new opportunities for making money and also the political life of the province. *Single faction dominance* became common. This concentration of wealth and power is a root cause of the persistence of inequality at the provincial level.

This chapter examines the factors and processes behind the emergence of single faction dominance in one province. The first section tracks how, up to the 1970s, political influence and opportunities for accumulating wealth were fragmented among several leading figures. The second section traces how one faction rose to dominance over the period from the 1970s to the 1990s. The faction first accumulated wealth, especially through the super profits available in businesses that were either illegal or organized as monopolies under government-granted concessions. This wealth was then leveraged to establish political power through networking and "influence," meaning power not recognized by law or custom, including the use of violence. Political power was then in turn leveraged for another round of wealth accumulation in which the faction shifted its investments away from the "black" or "grey" economy into legal businesses.

By the 1990s, this single faction dominated the local economy, particularly the province's major sector of tourism, and the construction industry. This faction also dominated politics from the national level (the election of MPs) down to village heads and the new institutions of decentralized local government. The faction also dominated the public life of the province through social work and charitable activities.

In the early 2000s, however, this single faction dominance came under challenge, as described in the third section. The background to this challenge can be traced to the impact of globalization on the local economy and of decentralization on local politics. The challenge came both from the inside—allies of the faction splitting away—and from the outside—new players with roots outside the province. In a very short time, the faction's control of the national and local levels of politics was undermined. Even so, the faction was able to recover by effecting some major changes in its business and political strategies. Although it is too soon to pass judgment, single faction dominance may possibly still continue.

The final section of this chapter examines the significance of this case from the angle of political economy.

For confidentiality, the name of the province is not mentioned, and the principal figure is disguised as "Mr K."

Multiple Power Centers until the 1970s

Until the 1970s, political power at the national level was highly centralized in the capital under the structure created by administrative reforms in the late 19th century, and this power was largely wielded by a bureaucratic elite of military, police and civilian officials under the system that Fred Riggs (1966) called a "bureaucratic polity."

In the province under study in this era, there were several powerful groups, all of a similar type with four main characteristics. First, the center of each group was a local capitalist who had risen from humble origins. Second, his major profits came from illegal or semi-legal businesses. Third, his economic success was built and protected by extensive use of informal power or "influence," including the use of violence. In local terminology, such figures were known as *jao pho* or "godfathers." Fourth, he established relations with powerful figures in the national capital that gave him both protection and business opportunities.

Long Ju K, who came to prominence in the 1950s and 1960s, was a Chinese immigrant who began with a sugar plantation, and accumulated enough to open a sugar mill. He then invested the profits in a rice mill, saw mill, mines, orchards, and land (Sumali 2000: 123; Pasuk and Sangsit 1994: 207). Long Ju K built relationships with powerful figures in the central state including the police chief Phao Siriyanon, prime minister Thanom Kittikachon, and General Sudsai Thepsadin. With this protection, he was able to enter businesses under government-granted concessions, and to expand his businesses into neighboring provinces, acquiring saw mills, rice mills, sugar plantations and antimony mining concessions. After Long Ju K was killed in a road accident in 1967, his network was challenged by rivals. His descendants tried to maintain influence but were all assassinated (Sumali 2000: 182; Pasuk and Sangsit 1994: 207).

Sia J rose to prominence after Long Ju K's death. He began as a bus driver and conductor, became a pork vendor, and opened a slaughterhouse. However, his major accumulation came from various illegal businesses. He invested the profits in a saw mill, rice mill, petrol stations, hotel, liquor agency and land. He became an influential figure by distributing businesses among dependents in his network (Pasuk and Sangsit 1994: 208). He also accumulated social capital by supporting the Village Scouts and becoming its local head, and developed a political role by acting as a vote-broker for many local and national politicians. His network collapsed after Sia J was assassinated in the early 1980s, and his descendants met the same fate as those of Long Ju K (Sondhi 2003).

Sia H began as a fertilizer trader, but then married the daughter of a large-scale agriculturist who became an MP of the province. Subsequently he opened an auto dealership and went into mining and then land dealing. He developed relationships with both local officials and national leaders, and also began to build social capital by giving money for social projects and many charities, such as a four million baht donation to build a ward for a hospital. His influence was initially confined to a single district. He attempted to expand beyond this district by bidding successfully on a construction project for a shopping center in another district, but this move sparked conflict with the influential businessmen of that district. Sia H was assassinated in the late 1980s.

The development of Mr K's single faction dominance dates from the violent collapse of these three networks in the 1980s.

The Emergence of Single Faction Dominance

Capital Accumulation and Power Networks in the Era of Black-grey Business

Mr K came from a Chinese immigrant family that settled in a village of the province. He went to school for four years then began work as a bus boy, rising to conductor, and then driver. He left to become a company employee and rose to become an entrepreneur in the same business. As soon as he had some financial security, he entered the political world by standing for election as a village headman in the 1960s, and becoming a vote-broker for a national politician, helping him to become an MP for the province.

His business was organized on the *kongsi* model, meaning that the family had joint ownership of the business assets, while the senior member of the family had total managerial control. In his early years, many of his business interests were illegal or semi-legal, including smuggling, gambling, and various activities connected to the entertainment industry. His business methods also veered into illegality, including the threat or use of violence. He built his business and political network through personal connections (interviews 13, 15, 22).

The turning point in Mr K's early career came when he met a French businessman who had businesses in Cambodia and who invited Mr K to meet the deputy prime minister of Cambodia. In the early 1970s, the Cambodian government allotted a quota for fishing boats in Cambodian territorial waters. Through this connection, Mr K acquired a license to travel in Cambodian coastal waters without supervision and control of officials. Mr K began to combine fishing and smuggling. After a few years of rapid accumulation, he quit fishing and concentrated on the construction business, including project contracts and securing concessions to run a laterite quarry and sell earth for landfill. The construction business depended heavily on contracts from government agencies acquired through connections and kickbacks (Pasuk and Sangsit 1994: 209; Viengrat 1988: 83–4; Sinthuchai 1996: 130–1).

As Mr K's growing wealth was now making him a prominent figure, Sia J encouraged him to play a larger role in politics. He attained the post of *kamnan* (sub-district head) in the mid-1970s without anyone daring to stand against him. He became a vote-broker for several politicians in the province, helped some to be elected as MPs, and thus gained growing influence in the capital. From here, he expanded his business interests into hotels and a liquor agency. He founded many companies, not only as tools of business, but also as a way to expand local influence by distributing business opportunities and profits to people in his network, such as other *kamnan*, village headmen, and district notables, particularly by offering them sub-agencies of the liquor business (Sinthuchai 1996: 182–3; Sombat 1992; interviews 1, 11).

Leveraging Wealth into Power

As his reputation and network became well known in both business and political circles, he encouraged his relatives and people in his business network to enter the political world, and began to invade the turf of one of the senior figures in the province's politics. In the late 1980s he had a major political success when a relative became a minister. With the combination of his official position, unofficial influence, and money power, he began to establish the dominance of a single network (interviews 1, 4, 16).

Mr K's political network at this stage consisted mostly of *kamnan*, village headmen, local-level politicians, and health volunteers. He nurtured this network in several ways. He encouraged an in-law to become president of the province's association of *kamnan* and headmen. He sent several dependents to contest in local government elections. He captured construction contracts under the provincial allocation from the national budget, and distributed these among his allies. Within the network there was a convention that projects valued above 100 million baht would be allocated to Mr K's own companies, but smaller projects were distributed among local politicians in the network. Opportunities in various grey businesses were allocated on similar principles (interview 3; Chaiyon and Olarn 2007: 14).

Mr K also concentrated on building relationships with officials, at two levels. If central officials visited the province, Mr K would arrange to meet them and lobby for completion of projects in the provincial plan (interview 3). With local officials, he shared benefits. For example, at first an official would patronize Mr K by offering protection, and subsequently Mr K would reward the official with money or other recompense. Mr K was quoted as saying, "If a senior official comes and asks to change his car, I must buy one for him." Subsequently as Mr K gained more influence in the central government through his political contacts, he was able to exercise influence over both local and national officials. Another major turning point came when Mr K was able to use his influence through the ruling party of the time to have someone appointed as the provincial governor (Sinthuchai 1996: 145–7; interview 4).

At first Mr K took care not to intrude onto the interests of two influential groups that remained. In both politics and business, they divided up the space for mutual benefit. Meanwhile Mr K forged horizontal relations with parallel networks in neighboring provinces, including their godfathers and godmothers (interviews 2, 13, 18).

Mr K paid special attention to the military which had two important units stationed in the province. With one, Mr K was able to develop a personal relationship with an officer because he had acted as that officer's driver when Mr K had been a conscript soldier. Mr K managed to divert the local government budget to construct a reservoir in the military base, and provided construction machinery for building roads and landscaping on the base (interviews 9, 19).

Mr K used his political influence to aid other business groups. For example, he "cleared the way" for one group to establish an industrial estate, and provided financial help when another large business group was in trouble. The latter repaid the favor by giving several construction contracts in the industrial estate to Mr K's companies, and by helping Mr K's network to establish a political party (interviews 5, 11).

Mr K also cultivated relations with a university within the province, particularly through its rector. When this rector was ousted by student demonstrations, Mr K cut his links with the university, but later decided to revive the relationship. A close associate of Mr K became head of the Provincial Administrative Organization which then provided the budget to build several facilities inside the university (interview 21).

Mr K also gradually accumulated some social capital through charity and social activities. He donated large sums to assist the poor through education and subsistence, provided bail money for suspects, negotiated with officials in cases of conflict with local people, and funded public facilities and charities including *wat* buildings and provincial government offices. He donated money for local development projects, and donated land to accommodate a village of over a hundred households after the municipality had evicted the village to build a municipal office.

Mr K's wife also had an important role in building social networks, especially through women's groups She became chairwoman of the provincial woman's development committee, which also had responsibility for activities concerning children, youth and the elderly, and which reached down into the localities through a network of women's groups.

Leveraging Political Power to Bring Business above Ground

The development of a wide network across business, officialdom, politics, and society was a condition for Mr K to make a transition from "black" or "grey" businesses to "white" ones (Viengrat 1988: 85; Sinthuchai 1996: 153). At first, he focused his legal interests on one municipality that was developing as a tourist resort, and gradually invested in several legitimate businesses connected to the tourist trade. Later when the national government earmarked part of the province as a zone of industrial development, Mr K became a broker in land for industry. The land business was highly profitable as the margins were wide. One plot bought for 300 million baht was sold for 900 million baht. Another plot sold to an industrial estate was bought for 90,000 baht per rai and sold for 170,000 baht per rai. In the tourist zone, Mr K bought one plot at 40,000 baht per rai and sold it for over 10 million baht per rai (Sinthuchai 1996: 160).

The government's promotion of industry in the province also boosted Mr K's construction contracting business including filling land and building basic infrastructure. In addition, business groups investing in industry in this province for the first time sought to build good relations with Mr K's network by awarding construction contracts. Foreign investors who needed to show a certain percentage of Thai ownership in their capital structure to meet legal requirements often made arrangements to use Mr K's name for this purpose (Chaiyon and Olarn 2006: 44–6; Sondhi 2003).

The Emergence of Single Faction Dominance

Mr K's network was built brick by brick over a long period, gradually engrossing more of the business opportunities and occupying more of the political space. From the mid-1990s, the dominance of a single faction emerged. Another key turning point occurred when Mr K moved his network under the umbrella of one national political party, and people in his network won a convincing victory in elections to the national legislature (interviews 14, 20). As a reward for its contribution to the national victory by this political party, the faction was awarded a deputy minister post. Probably not by chance, the post was in the Ministry of Industry. At the next general election, Mr K's network again swept the province's seats. This time the reward was a full ministerial post.

Mr K was now such a significant force in politics that his influence overflowed the borders of the province. Mr K was able to use his political influence to raise an ally to become chairman of the Provincial Administrative Organization in a neighboring province, to have another ally elected as the province's senator, and to become important as a mediator between conflicting groups in the province (Chaiyon and Olarn 2006: 52).

From the late 1990s, decentralization had a major impact on the structure of politics in the provinces. New elective local government bodies were created at the level of the province and subdistrict; several new municipalities (already elective) were created; and a share of the national budget was devolved onto these bodies.

In response, Mr K adjusted his local network. Whereas before he had concentrated on building links with *kamnan* and village heads, he now focused on politicians in local government bodies. He was able to place allies in almost every local government body in the province (Natasha 1997: 110). If Mr K's network supported a local government candidate, that person would get elected by the local people every time. Such candidates displayed Mr K's support by including a picture of Mr K with the candidate on their election poster, or including a symbol of the network. Local politicians at all levels sought his support to the point that there arose a saying, "though all roads lead to Rome, in this province politicians have to head towards Mr K."

Another innovation of this era was the creation of popular assemblies (*prachakhom*) to give civil society an informal voice in local politics, particularly for evaluating and approving local development plans. Mr K was able to send his people to head these popular assemblies (interview 17).

From Single Party Dominance to Business Expansion

Political dominance was then the foundation for a further expansion of business investment by Mr K and the allies in his network.

Mr K expanded his investments in the hotel industry, including investing over 300 million baht in a new luxury hotel, and another 400 million baht in upgrading existing hotels under the network. As a result of rapid growth in the province's economy and Mr K's close links to the ruling party in the national government, the flow of construction contracts to the group greatly increased. In particular, the network was awarded projects of waste disposal and waste water disposal in many locations. To handle this work, the network created many new construction companies. In this period, the group bid for contracts on large government projects worth over two billion baht (interview 7). In addition, network companies succeeded in bids for constructing a port and a railway line, as well as a tugboat business in the local port.

Mr K played a leading role in organizing a ring of construction contractors to share out contracts on a queuing system (*hua pramun*). In the case of the construction of a bridge for the Provincial Administrative Organization at a cost of 600 million baht, Mr K presided over negotiations for other contractors to withdraw from the bidding in favor of a company in the network, for which service he received a reward of 7 million baht (interview 7).

In this period, Mr K tried to associate himself with national-level capital that wanted to invest in service businesses in the province. When a group proposed to build a racetrack in the province, Mr K announced that he would provide a plot of 600 rai for the project. When another group proposed a major entertainment center, Mr K gave support on grounds the project would increase the prosperity of the province (*Matichon*, Apr. 17, 2003).

Summary: Single Faction Dominance

From bus-boy to *kamnan*, from fisherman-smuggler to major construction contractor and land dealer, Mr K's wealth expanded in parallel with a growing role in national and local politics. He started as a vote-broker and gradually developed a political network that ranged from relatives sitting in the parliament and cabinet down to local government bodies and village heads. His economic power, political links, social capital, and extra-legal "influence" gave him a virtually monopolistic position in the province's politics and in the province's economy, especially its service sector including construction contracting for the public and private sectors. Mr K is an example of a local figure who accumulated capital and built his economic power to a certain level where he could leverage his economic strength to create a powerful political network, and then exploited his political position to further strengthen his economic base. His access to social resources and his domination of politics resulted in growing wealth. When a television interviewer in the late 1990s asked about his wealth in the form of property and other assets, Mr K estimated that its total value was over 10 billion baht (interview with Mr K on ITV, n.d.).

The Challenge to Single Faction Dominance

Although Mr K's network seemed to be one of the most dominant networks at the provincial level in the whole country, in the mid-2000s it was suddenly undermined. There were two killer blows.

First, a new business group triumphed at national elections. Mr K had built his business and his political influence inside the province from the ground up. This new business group came from above and from outside. It arrived along with the entry of large-scale national-level capital into the province as a result of the government's policy of industrial development. Mr K had become expert at dealing with local rivals by either running them out of town or folding them into his own network. But these tactics were ineffective against a new group whose financial and political power was located outside the province, in the national capital.

Second, Mr K was removed from the scene as a result of a major court case over his use of "influence" to build his wealth and political power. Without his authority, influence, wealth and connections, the single faction dominance was challenged by several groups, including breakaway factions, old rivals and new players in the province (*Matichon Sutsapda* 26, 1339, Apr. 14–20, 2006: 97–8). The next generation of Mr K's family had to assume the leadership quite suddenly. At first they were able to retain the support of groups in the network, but before long cracks began to show. The instability of the network resulted from the breaking of its central pillar as well as conflict between constituent groups (interviews 12, 16).

As the network crumbled, two new centers of power emerged. One included politicians from an old political party along with local officials and breakaways from Mr K's network. Another group consisted mainly of new businessmen with outside connections and strong links to the military (interviews 6, 10, 14, 16, 18).

The network's decline was revealed when it lost the monopoly on MP seats that it had commanded for two decades. At the polls in 2007, the network lost to the first new group running under the banner of a rival party. Both groups also challenged the network's hold on local politics, inflicting defeats in elections for the mayor of several of the province's urban areas (Phujatkan Online, Mar. 10, 2008).

The network was caught in a crisis of transition. Whereas Mr K had come from humble origins, his successors had gained higher education, finishing with degrees from overseas. Whereas Mr K had operated in a very lax environment, public tolerance for use of violence had diminished, and Mr K's successors were loath to use methods that prejudiced their attempt to build a new image for the network (interview 3).

Readjustment and Recovery

The Mr K network reacted by shifting both their business practice and their political strategy away from the old use of influence and personal connections towards something more above-board and more institutionalized.

The new leaders of the network paid more attention to local-level politics. Although Mr K had placed allies in major government bodies, many of these had been displaced by the new rivals. As the budget handled by local government bodies had significantly increased, these bodies had greater importance for any local political network. Mr K network signaled its change of strategy when a member of the family, whose role to that point had been to look after the business side of the family, won election as mayor of a major municipality (interview 8).

The new leaders also paid more attention to the cultural aspects of politics. They increasingly relied upon cultural activities, rather than "influence," to expand their electoral base and build legitimacy. They became more involved in sport, tourism promotion, and traditional cultural activities. Their major focus was football, which was enjoying a boom of popularity. One member of the group said in a magazine interview that a portion of the votes that brought victory in elections now came from fans of the football club which the group sponsored.

In 2010, the new leaders founded their own political party to compete in national elections to show local people that the party's main object would be working for the benefit of the province rather than serving the interests of national leaders from outside.

These strategies revived the fortunes of the faction. The cracks in the network were healed and unity reestablished. In 2011, Mr. K's network again won victory at the national election, and again was offered a ministerial post in the subsequent government. At local elections too, the network successfully won back from rivals in many places, and controlled virtually all the important local government bodies. Whether the single faction dominance will be as solid and sustainable as in the time of Mr K himself remains to be seen.

Conclusion: Towards Equity in Local Society

The single faction dominance constructed by Mr K over the period from the 1970s to the 2000s is a rather extreme form of a tendency that is present in many of Thailand's provinces. The ability to construct dominance arose from three principal conditions: the weak state of the rule of law that permitted illegal and semi-legal businesses to flourish, and that allowed the use or threat of violence with impunity; a high degree of centralization of power in the central government which meant that powerful connections to the center gave both protection and privileges; and the existence of monopolistic or concession-based businesses, including construction, that could be captured by political means and that delivered very high levels of profit. In this environment, Mr K's network could practice primitive accumulation, convert wealth into power, and leverage power for more wealth. The three factions that dominated the province earlier had used the same model. Mr K was able to consolidate and expand the scale of the operation. In part this was possible simply because he had a long career (he started very young) and had a large and fairly unified family which gave him the time and the management resources for this expansion of scale.

Such concentration of wealth and power in a single family and its personal network contributes to inequality by restricting the opportunities available to everybody else.

How far have the conditions that framed Mr K's rise (weak rule of law, centralization of power, monopoly businesses) changed in recent decades?

The fact that Mr K was neutralized by a criminal case suggests there has been some advance in the rule of law, but care should be taken not to exaggerate the extent. The case affected Mr K alone and did not damage the network, which managed to make a rapid recovery from the crisis.

Decentralization to elective local government has been a major change in the structure of the state, but again the impact should not be exaggerated. Mr K's faction was able to "manage" the arrival of the new elective bodies by adapting its old methods. This is partly because decentralization has been limited. The transfer of power and budget to the local bodies has failed to meet the original targets. The central ministries have been reluctant to see their powers diminished, and hence political connections into the central state are still important.

Further decentralization is a necessary condition for greater equity in local affairs but not a sufficient condition. There must also be a more equitable distribution of power within the locality, through further decentralization at both national and local levels. Civil society organizations need greater weight. The civic assemblies begun in recent years need to become more independent from the old mechanisms of patronage politics. A culture of democratic participation needs to be developed over the long term by using the momentum of growing appreciation of the opportunity presented by democratic decentralization.

The importance of concession-based businesses has diminished with the disappearance of the liquor monopoly and similar arrangements. But construction contracting on projects funded from public budgets remains a business that can be converted into a highly profitable monopoly through the exercise of political power and influence. Measures are needed to ensure greater public scrutiny of this sector.

The crisis that undermined Mr K's faction in the 2000s shows that the environment of provincial politics has begun to change. The faction's ability to recover by shifting towards more modern methods of both business and politics confirms this trend of change. But the extent of change should not be exaggerated. The inequities in power and economic opportunity at the provincial level will diminish significantly only when advances in the rule of law and democratic decentralization make *single faction dominance* no longer possible.

Note

1. This chapter is based on hundreds of interviews conducted over a 20-year span with local politicians, government officials, businessmen, teachers and activists. On legal advice, the names of the province and the key actors have been disguised. For obvious reasons, the sources cannot be disclosed. The principal interviews are listed in the References.

References

Books and Articles

Chaiyon Praditsil and Olarn Thinbangtieo. 2006. *Botbat thang kan mueang khong jao pho thongthin nai krasae lokaphiwat: korani sueksa jangwat nueng thang phak tawanok* [Political Role of Local Godfathers under Globalization: Case Study of an Eastern Province]. Research study under project on Thai capital after the crisis.

———. 2007. *Khrongsang amnat kap kan khap khluean khrongkan thang sangkhom* [Power Structure and the Progress of Social Projects]. Bangkok: Thailand Research Fund.

McVey, Ruth. 2000. *Money and Power in Provincial Thailand.* Copenhagen: Nordic Institute of Asian Studies.

Natasha Wasindilok. 1997. "Khrongsang amnat nai chumchon kap kan mueang thongthin" [Power Structure and Local Politics]. MA thesis, Chulalongkorn University, Bangkok.

Pasuk Phongpaichit and Sangsit Piriyarangsan. 1994. *Khorrapchan kap prachathippattai* [Corruption and Democracy]. Bangkok: Political Economy Center, Chulalongkorn University.

Riggs, F.W. 1966. *Thailand: The Modernization of a Bureaucratic Polity.* Honolulu: East West Center Press.

Sinthuchai Sukorasep. 1996. "Botbat khong jao pho nai kan mueang thai 2517–2535" [Role of Godfathers in Thai Politics 1976–1992]. MA thesis, Chulalongkorn University.

Sombat Chantornwong. 1992. "Botbat khong jao pho thongthin nai sethakit lae kan mueang thai: kho sanget boeng ton" [Role of Local Godfathers in the Thai Economy and Politics: Primary Considerations]. In *Rat thun jao pho thongthin kap sangkhom thai* [State, Capital, and Local Godfathers in Thai Society], ed. Pasuk Phongpaichit and Sangsit Piriyarangsan. Bangkok: Chulalongkorn University.

Sondhi Limthongkul. 2003. "Kut rak heng jao pho" [Digging up the Roots of the Godfathers]. Interview on program, *Sapha tha phra athit*, FM 97.5, Apr. 11.

Sumali Phanyura. 2000. "Phatthanakan khong amnat thongthin nai boriwen lumnam bang pakong lae chai fung thale tawan ok pho so 2440–2516" [Development of Local Power in the Bang Pakong River Basin and Eastern Coast, 1897–1973]. MA thesis, Chulalongkorn University.

UNDP. 2014 *Thailand Human Development Report 2014: Advancing Human Development through the ASEAN Community.* Bangkok: UNDP.

Viengrat Nethipo. 1982. "Thurakit nakleng + nakleng thurakit = nak thurakit kueng nakleng" [Mafia Business + Business Mafia = Semi-Businessman Semi-Mafia]. *Jotmai khao sangkhomsat* [*Social Science White Papers*] 11, 1: 82–103.

Interviews

1. Former MP of study province, Sept. 21, 2009
2. Former MP of study province, Apr. 28, 2010
3. Former university rector and senator, Aug. 14, 2010
4. Former MP of study province, Sept. 20, 2009
5. Chairman of tambon municipality, June 1, 2011
6. Former Democrat Party MP of the study province, Feb. 12, 2010
7. Officer of the provincial mechanics group, Oct. 5, 2010
8. Anonymous interview, Aug. 5, 2010
9. Anonymous interview, Sept. 30, 2011
10. MP for the study province, Aug. 28, 2010

11. Member of the Provincial Administrative Organization, Sept. 30, 2011
12. Former chairman of the Provincial Administrative Organization, July 28, 2009
13. Municipal councilor, associate of Mr K, Oct. 8, 2010
14. Democrat MP for the study province, Sept. 8, 2010
15. Anonymous interview, Sept. 12, 2009
16. Former MP of study province, Aug. 7, 2010
17. Former chairman of people's municipal assembly, Jan. 30, 2010
18. Democrat MP of the study province, Sept. 12, 2010
19. Anonymous interview, July 30, 2011
20. Former MP of the study province and former Senate speaker, Sept. 8, 2011
21. Anonymous interview, Sept. 30, 2011
22. Former university rector and senator, Aug. 7, 2010

8

Network Thaksin: Structure, Roles and Reaction

UKRIST PATHMANAND

Thaksin Shinawatra made a fortune of US$2 billion, won two general elections by the largest majorities seen in Thailand, and was the first civilian premier to last a full term. Even after he was ejected by a coup on September 19, 2006 and went into self-exile to evade a prison sentence, he continued to have influence over three governments headed by his relatives or nominees.[1] After his political party had been disbanded twice, after the constitution had been re-written to change the balance of power, and over five years after Thaksin had last set foot in the country, a movement still took to the streets with the stated aim "to eradicate the Thaksin regime." Only after yet another coup in May 2014 did his opponents feel confident that this objective might be attained.

In the past, coups and exile have brought a decisive end to several Thai political figures. The fact that Thaksin proved so difficult to "eradicate" is testament to the extraordinary nature of his political influence. What exactly was the "Thaksin regime"? How did it work? Why did it survive so long? What does its rise and long fall tell us about the distribution of political power?

The networks that bind many groups together have become an essential element of Thai politics, arguably more important than formal institutions. Over his career at the center of Thai politics, Thaksin constructed two neworks. The first, begun in the late 1990s and early 2000s, included big business groups, provincial politicians, and elements from the army and the police. Apart from the front-line prominence of big business figures, who normally preferred a more veiled political role, this network was only marginally different from others seen in the recent past. Thaksin had support from the mass electorate, but initially this did not seem different from his predecessors. As noted in Chapter 1, the power structure of Thailand can be described as a "flexible oligarchy" that is responsive to the need to incorporate new centers of influence. Thaksin's first network was not immediately seen to transgress the limits of that flexibility. As a result, Thaksin won strong electoral support in Bangkok at the 2001 elections, was given support from elite quarters to face down charges of corruption, and generally enjoyed elite support in the early 2000s.

Thaksin's second network, constructed after he was overthrown by a military coup in 2006, was very different. Most of the big businessmen who had supported Thaksin in expectation he would help them recover from the 1997 financial crisis had quietly withdrawn. The few big businessmen remaining were close and loyal friends. Many police and military who had been his friends at the cadet school or subordinates in the police also withdrew, and those in uniform that remained were already retired or no longer on active service. They no longer functioned to block the elements in the armed forces that were opposed to Thaksin. Grassroots supporters had become the core of Thaksin's network. Local politicians, local community leaders, and middle-level businessmen in provincial areas had become the main nodes in the network. Media played a new role in binding this network together. The network had begun to have a life of its own, independent of Thaksin, though he remained important as its political inspiration as well as a source of finance.

This second network had not only reached beyond the limits of "flexible oligarchy," but in many ways was opposed to the principle of oligarchy itself. The campaign to overthrow this second network extended over almost eight years and involved judicial activism, prolonged street demonstrations, and eventually another coup. Two conclusions emerge from this long and bitter struggle. First, the oligarchy was prepared to mobilize many different weapons and go to great lengths to eradicate Network Thaksin. Second, Network Thaksin showed extraordinary staying power in the face of this onslaught.

The first section of this chapter looks at the first version of Network Thaksin constructed from the late 1990s while the second examines the second version that emerged after the 2006 coup. The conclusion reflects on the implications of Thaksin's rise and fall.

Network Thaksin before the 2006 Coup

Both the political structure and personal factors contributed to the rise of Network Thaksin. The constitution of 1997 was designed to create a strong executive. The party list system of election, introduced by this constitution, allowed many big businessmen to become MPs. The upsurge of interest in politics in the provincial areas created a new kind of electoral base. Against this background, a businessman turned politician like Thaksin was able to become prime minister and retain influence over a long period. His own leadership skills, speaking ability, and business-style decisiveness also contributed to his political success.

But apart from structural and personal factors, Thaksin's ability to create a power network that involved both important elite groups and the grassroots mass was crucial to his rise. Such network power is not unique in Thailand, but had not been seen on such a scale since the 1980s. His predecessors as prime minister—Chuan Leekpai, Banharn Silapa-archa, and General Chavalit Yongchaiyudh—had no equivalent network, were leaders of coalition governments with no strong majority, and failed to complete a single full term in office.[2]

The only comparable political network seen in the past three decades is the special case of General Prem Tinsulanond, who was army commander-in-chief (1979–81) and minister of defense (1980–81) before holding the position of premier for eight years (1980–88). His power network, however, was created in the conditions known as "semi-democracy," under which bureaucrats had more influence than elected politicians, and both the army and the political parties were weak. Civilian leaders of political parties stood aside and allowed General Prem to become premier. In his study of "Network Monarchy," Duncan McCargo (2005) proposed that General Prem was the key figure in a network that extended outward and downward from the charisma of the king via the privy councilors and prominent military figures to all his loyal subjects.

The roots of Network Thaksin, along with its structure and consequences for Thai society, differ from that of Prem. Before rising to become prime minister in 2001, Thaksin had rather little political experience. He was minister of foreign affairs for 100 days in the first Chuan Leekpai government (1992–95), and became leader of the Palang Tham Party for a short time in 1995 before setting up the

Thai Rak Thai Party in July 1998. But from 2001 onwards, Thaksin developed his own power network that included several large business groups, political parties, and some elements in the army and police.

The Formation

While the network power of General Prem came from established political forces, that of Thaksin arose from the new economic and political structure around the turn of the millennium in which large business groups had roles in politics through political parties and parliament. The crucial turning point came in 1997 with the coincidence of the Asian financial crisis and the passing of a new constitution. The financial crisis radically changed the structure and composition of large business groups in Thailand. Many companies were crippled by debt and forced into bankruptcy. Across many sectors of the economy including banking, industry and large-scale retailing, there were major changes in ownership. Multinational companies acquired larger stakes. Even among the Thai business groups that weathered the storm and survived, companies had to be restructured and reorganized (Hewison 2004; Pasuk and Baker 2008). Those saddled with huge debts sought many different solutions, including help from the state through political means.

At the same time the 1997 constitution increased the power of the premier, and introduced the party-list system of election that gave businessmen and other elite figures an easier route for admission to parliament. The 1997 constitution also created many new independent organizations designed to monitor the government and parliament, including the National Counter Corruption Commission, the Election Commission, the Constitutional Court and the National Broadcasting and Telecommunications Commission (McCargo 2002).

The impact of the financial crisis and the 1997 constitution brought about a realignment of political groups and power relations. In particular, wealthy politicians and owners of large business conglomerates had more scope to enter politics and play leading roles without having to rely on old power groups in the army and the bureaucracy, as had been the case until then. The person who most clearly recognized and grasped this new situation was Thaksin Shinawatra.

Big Business Groups

On July 14, 1998, Thaksin registered his Thai Rak Thai Party and announced that this was the first party under the new constitution, aiming to work for the benefits of Thai society.[3] Financially the party was dependent on Thaksin's family and friends as he said in his speech in the annual party meeting in 2000 before the general election that,[4]

> I have asked permission from my wife to use the family money for my political work, so why would I use their money to destroy their reputation? So do not fear my wealthy status at all. Follow my deeds and see if I lied, see how I behave....

After Thai Rak Thai had won the 2001 election, he told the annual party meeting in April 2001,[5]

> I have received enough from this land and for another 50 years. If I lived to be 100, I would dedicate my body, mind, brain, all my strength and time to the nation. Therefore I am willing to use the money I have earned personally to lead a political party to be one that the people could pin their hope before the political reform could take over completely. I am ready and willing. There are many, many friends who use their own wealth without making troubles for the family to help make this party to be a party without corruption....

Before the appearance of Thaksin's Thai Rak Thai Party, big businessmen had supported political parties from behind the scenes, never openly. That now changed. Leading business owners in the sectors of telecommunications, banking, petrochemicals, steel, real estate and entertainment gave open support to Thaksin. Representatives of some groups became party-list MPs, took up important posts in the party, and served as cabinet ministers between 2001 and 2006. The premier thus became the centre of both economic and political power in Thailand in a way that had not been seen since the demise of the absolute monarchy in 1932. These big business groups formed the apex of a strategic pyramid of political strategy, or an "inner circle" of Thai Rak Thai (Figure 8.1).

The telecommunication groups in the network included Thaksin's own Shin Corporation, the largest operator of mobile phones; Telecom Asia belonging to the Charoen Pokphand group, the largest operator of landlines; TT&T Jasmine, another telecommunication giant whose owner, Adisai Photaramik, became commerce minister in

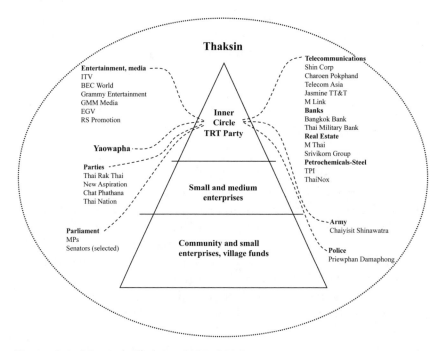

Thaksin

Entertainment, media
ITV
BEC World
Grammy Entertainment
GMM Media
EGV
RS Promotion

Inner
Circle
TRT Party

Yaowapha

Parties
Thai Rak Thai
New Aspiration
Chat Phathana
Thai Nation

Small and medium
enterprises

Parliament
MPs
Senators (selected)

Community and small
enterprises, village funds

Telecommunications
Shin Corp
Charoen Pokphand
Telecom Asia
Jasmine TT&T
M Link
Banks
Bangkok Bank
Thai Military Bank
Real Estate
M Thai
Srivikorn Group
Petrochemicals-Steel
TPI
ThaiNox

Army
Chaiyisit Shinawatra

Police
Priewphan Damaphong

Figure 8.1 Network Thaksin, 1997–2006

Thaksin's government; and M Link, a joint venture between Thaksin's sister Yaowapha Wongsawat and Suriya Juengrungroengkit, secretary-general of the Thai Rak Thai Party and minister of transport and communications.

The banking groups in the pyramid of power included the largest bank, Bangkok Bank, and the Thai Military Bank, a medium size bank in which members of Thaksin's family held a majority of the shares.

Industrial groups included Prachai Liaophairat's Thai Petrochemical Industries, a petrochemical conglomerate with a debt overhang of over 100,000 million baht;[6] and Prayuth Mahakitsiri's Thai Knox Steel, which had a debt overhang of almost one billion baht. Prayuth, who became deputy party head and a party-list MP, also owned a golf course which Thaksin patronized, and became a significant recipient of government assistance during Thaksin's term when the government-owned Krung Thai Bank reduced the group's debt burden.

Several real estate groups were part of the core. The Thai M Group was owned by Suchai Veeramethikul, whose youngest son Veerachai was a founder member of Thai Rak Thai Party and became an advisor to the minister of foreign affairs and chairman of the parliamentarian subcommittee on finance and banking. Chalermphan Srivikorn of the Srivikorn group had once been secretary general of the Democrat Party but had quit after losing a factional struggle in the early 1990s. His son, Phimon, became secretary to Thaksin's minister of finance, Somkid Jatusripitak. Phimon's mother, Khunying Sasima Srivikorn, was appointed a member of the Thai Airways board of directors.

Entertainment groups had not been involved in politics before. They provided important help to Thaksin in the form of advertising, event services and political campaigning. Paibul Damrongchaitham, owner of Grammy Entertainment, had been a member of Thaksin's inner coterie for more than ten years. When Thaksin was charged with concealing his assets in August 2001, Paibul had given him moral support.[7] Pracha Maleenont of BEC World, a company that held the concession to operate popular TV Channel 3, was placed tenth on Thai Rak Thai's party list, and became deputy minister of transport and communications, taking charge of Thai Airways. Thaksin also bought up iTV, the first independent TV channel, and maintained close links with other entertainment groups such as RS Promotion. These groups provided assistance in open ways, such as when Grammy made available its performers and artists to give public support to government activities including an anti-drug campaign and tourism promotion, but also in covert ways such as bias in news coverage.

Military and Police: Relatives and Friends

Apart from big business groups, Thaksin's network power included alliances with the military in a way that no other civilian premier had been able to do. In the early period of his first government, Thaksin let all the decisions on military affairs be decided by General Chavalit Yongchaiyudh, minister of defence, General Yutthasak Sasiprapha, deputy defense minister, and General Thammarak Israngkura na Ayutthaya, minister of the Prime Minister Office. At a major military reshuffle in August 2001, he arranged the promotion of two former classmates from the Cadet School cadet class 10, Songkitti Chakkabat, to become deputy commander of the Fourth Army Region, and Suriyo Inbamrung as commander of the 33rd Infantry, both key posts in the region of Chiang Mai and Chiang Rai, even though neither had served in the area before. He also appointed two relatives, Uthai

Shinawatra as deputy director of the army's Office of Policy and Planning, and Chaiyasit Shinawatra as deputy commander of the Armed Forces Development Command.

In another reshuffle in September 2002, the commander-in-chief of the army, General Surayuth Chulanont, an officer close to General Prem Tinsulanond, was moved up to become Supreme Commander on grounds that his aggressive stance towards the government of Myanmar was a barrier to Thai-Myanmar relations. Myanmar had accused a special unit of the Thai army, created by General Surayuth in 2001 to counter the spread of drugs, of attacking the United Wa State Army, a minority group that cooperated with the Myanmar military (Thitinan 2003: 283). General Somthat Uttanand became the new army commander, while other Thaksin allies were boosted up the army hierarchy, including General Chaiyasit Shinawatra who became deputy army chief. Another 15 officers belonging to the same military cadet class as Thaksin were promoted upwards (McCargo and Ukrist 2005: 121–65). General Thammarak, an important core member of the Thai Rak Thai Party and a popular personality in the northeast, became minister of defense, and helped to move Thaksin's friends and colleagues into important positions including chief of the 4th Army Region, commander of the Fourth Cavalry, commander of the First Unit of the Royal Guard, and commander of the 11th Infantry. Eventually Chaiyasit was promoted to become army chief in September 2003. In all 35 members of military cadet class 10 took control of major posts in the army, navy and air force, as well as policy and budget positions in the Supreme Command, and the bureau of the under-secretary of the Ministry of Defense. Through this network of classmates and relatives, Thaksin took a strong grip on the military.

Thaksin tried to appease others in the military by allowing them to purchase arms.[8] At a meeting of all the military leaders on September 2, 2003, Thaksin agreed to increase the military procurement budget from 17 billion baht to 20 billion baht to buy arms and develop the military for the period 2005–13. He approved the army's plan to buy 33 Black Hawk helicopters, valued at 750 million baht; and supported the air force proposal to upgrade its F16 and F5 fighters.[9] When he took leaders of the army, navy and the air force to Russia in order to shop for arms and satellite projects,[10] he cited the King's words,

> His Majesty the King has said that the army had been short of budget for many years. But the soldiers must have potential and be ready for combat all the time.[11]

Building a network in the police was easier. Thaksin had many classmates and colleagues from his time in the police, now in the middle ranks, including his wife's two brothers who came from an established "police family" and were well-backed within the senior levels of the force. Still, Thaksin gave a little extra help. His brother-in-law Prieophan Damaphong was boosted to assistant national police chief in 2003 and then to deputy in 2004, bypassing more senior candidates.

Provincial Politicians

As Thaksin's political star rose in the late 1990s, several of the political bosses who dominated provincial Thailand hitched their wagons to this rising star. Six months before the 2001 election, around 100 sitting MPs from other parties had decided to run as Thai Rak Thai candidates at the coming poll, including 58 from the New Aspiration Party, 16 from Chat Phatthana, 11 from Social Action, 9 from Chat Thai, and 6 from the Democrats.[12] Several of the bosses who had not made this move were defeated at the poll by the groundswell of popular support for Thaksin. After Thaksin's victory, New Aspiration and two smaller parties merged into Thai Rak Thai (Pasuk and Baker 2009: 88–91, 95). In the run-up to the 2005 election, Thaksin threatened to exclude all coalition partners from his next government, persuading several provincial factions to hop into Thai Rak Thai. With virtually all the major provincial politicians outside the southern region now inside Thai Rak Thai, Thaksin won a landslide victory at the 2005 poll, losing only 30 of the 311 constituency seats in the north, northeast and central regions.

Network Thaksin after the 2006 Coup

The military overthrew Thaksin's government by coup on September 19, 2006. In the two and a half years following the coup, Thaksin's party was dissolved twice, over 300 of its members were banned from politics for five years, Thaksin took himself into self-exile to avoid a prison sentence, the courts froze and then seized almost two billion baht of his family assets, the military underwent several rounds of internal purges, and a new constitution was written in part to prevent the concentration of power that Thaksin has established. Under this attack, the Network Thaksin established over the previous decade was irretrievably damaged. Most of the big business families quietly distanced themselves from Thaksin and gave him no open support. Most of his allies in the military were assigned to posts where they commanded no men and had no prospects. Among the provincial politicians, the results were more mixed. Some quietly removed themselves from the network, but many remained loyal, not least because the electorates on which they depended remained fiercely loyal to Thaksin.

Over the years following the coup, the network was recreated but in a very different form. As the network's foundations in business, the uniformed services, and provincial politics weakened, the mass base of support assumed greater significance, and the media became critical in tying the network together.

The loyalty of the mass base meant that, despite the assault on Thaksin and his network, his political party was able to win elections in 2007 and 2011, ushering in pro-Thaksin governments. But these governments differed significantly from those before the coup.

Government by Nominee and Sibling

On May 30, 2007, a court dissolved the Thai Rak Thai Party and banned 111 of its executives from politics for five years. The party was quickly reincarnated under a new name as the People Power Party, and won a convincing victory at a general election held on December 23, 2007. But the change in the party went much deeper than the name. Thaksin persuaded the veteran politican Samak Sundaravej to come out of retirement to lead the party and become prime minister.[13] Samak had entered politics in 1968 as a member of the Democrat Party, and established his own Prachakon Thai Party in 1976. He was popular in Bangkok because of his pugnacious personality, displayed in radio shows that combined cooking and politics. In 2000, he had been elected mayor of Bangkok by a landslide, the first candidate to garner over a million votes in this poll. Thaksin wanted an outsider to lead the party to avoid conflicts among his supporters, and also wanted someone with seniority to deal with his political enemies. Samak announced that he would be a "nominee of Thaksin" and would pursue an amnesty for the 111 executives of the former Thai Rak Thai party who had been barred from politics for five years.

For other positions in the cabinet, Thaksin chose people who were close to him personally. His legal advisor, Noppadol Patthama, became foreign minister; Sompong Amornwiwat, a long-time friend from their hometown of Chiang Mai, became minister of justice; Chalerm Yubamrung, instrumental in giving him the satellite concession that became the basis of his great wealth, became minister of interior; Somchai Wongsawat, his brother-in-law, became deputy prime minister; and Yongyuth Tiyapairat, another close friend from Chiang Rai, became speaker of the parliament.

Some core party activists were also accommodated. Jatuporn Promphan and Manit Jitjan had prominent positions on the party list. Nattawut Saikuea became the government spokesman; Jakraphop Penkhair, spokesman in Thaksin's earlier government, became a minister of the prime minister office.

The 2006 coup leaders had established an Assets Scrutiny Committee that launched a judicial assault against Thaksin, his family and his party. The first objective of the Samak government was to parry this assault. The new ministers of justice and interior along with some high-level bureaucrats killed some of the cases, and tried to have the Assets Scrutiny Committee dissolved. Uncooperative officials were moved, including the police chief, while certain officials that had been sidelined after the coup were reinstated.

In the beginning, the Samak government had good relations with the army chief, Anupong Paochinda. Before the 2007 election, Anupong had said, "the army will have no political role even though the old group may be returned to power."[14] Anupong often traveled with Samak on official foreign trips. Possibly Anupong was biding his time until the annual military promotions in September 2008, when Samak supported Anupong to remain as army chief for another year. After that, the relationships between Samak and the army changed immediately, from apparent political alliance to greater distance.[15]

After Samak became prime minister, the anti-Thaksin coalition that had come together in 2005 as the People's Alliance for Democracy (PAD), often called the Yellow Shirts, returned to the streets with the aim of overthrowing the government. On August 26, 2008, the PAD seized Government House. Samak invoked the Emergency Act to counter the demonstration, but Anupong refused to make use of its powers, declaring, "I insist that the parliament should take more responsibility. The international community will not accept the military interference. A coup will bring more problems. Soldiers will not use guns to manage the protesters. Soldiers will use only batons, teargas, and water hoses."[16] Soon after, the Samak government was ousted on grounds that Samak had taken a fee for appearing on a television cooking program. He was replaced by Somchai Wongsawat, Thaksin's brother-in-law, who lasted only two months before the Constitutional Court again dissolved Thaksin's party in December, bringing the government down. The attempts by the Samak and Somchai governments to block the judicial assault on Network Thaksin had failed.

The ministers in the pro-Thaksin governments over 2007–08 were drawn primarily from Thaksin's personal coterie and the Red Shirts. The businessmen and local politicians that had been such a major part of Network Thaksin prior to the 2006 coup were largely absent. With a few exceptions, the big business owners had quietly distanced themselves from Thaksin. Most of the provincial politicians had initially remained loyal to Thaksin, but several had begun to ease away as the judicial assault gathered force.

After the Somchai government was undermined, a faction of pro-Thaksin MPs led by the Buriram boss, Newin Chidchob, was persuaded to defect, making it possible to form a new coalition headed by the Democrat Party. Since his entry into politics in the early 1990s, Newin had become one of the most prominent of the new wave of provincial politicians. His decision to join Thaksin shortly before the 2005 election had seemed to complete Thaksin's domination of provincial politicians outside the south. Newin's defection was equally significant as a measure of Thaksin's waning grip on this key part of his network.

Network Thaksin and the Red Shirts

The 2006 coup gave rise to a new coalition of all those who opposed the coup. This included some confirmed supporters of Thaksin, but also others who simply opposed the military intervention in politics. Naruemon Thapchumphon dubbed this combination "the anti anti Thaksin coalition."[17] In the first few months after the coup, various small groups held protests. In June, a coalition of these groups set up the United Front for Democracy against Dictatorship (UDD) to coordinate these activities. Around this time, the protesters began wearing red as an identifying uniform, and within months the grouping had been dubbed the "Red Shirts." The UDD attacked General Prem as

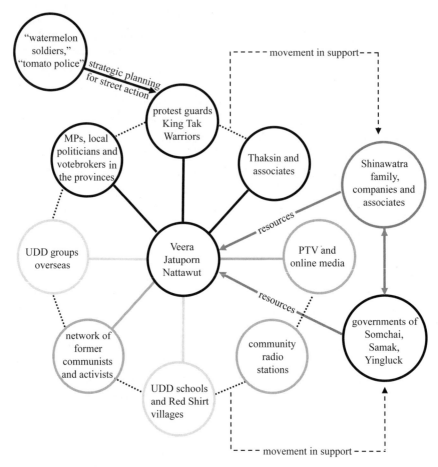

Figure 8.2 Network Thaksin after the 2006 Coup

"the man behind the coup" and attempted to collect 150,000 signatures to present a petition to the king to remove Prem from the Privy Council. On July 22, 2007, the UDD organized a march to Prem's house at Si Sao Theves, ending in a violent clash between the demonstrators and the police, resulting in many injuries.

Protest activities continued through 2007, reduced for a time after the installation of the Samak government in December, revived to counter Yellow Shirt protests in late 2008, and continued to mount from the downfall of the Somchai government in December 2008 to the violent confrontations in Bangkok in March–May 2010. In this new political context, Network Thaksin became very different from its earlier form. Primarily now it was an activist coalition. Thaksin was no longer its central pole, although he remained important as a symbol and as a source of funds. The center was now occupied by those who had the skills to run such an activist coalition. The network became much more complex as it took on the task of coordinating activities without much support of established institutions. Membership in the network became more varied, encompassing both followers of Thaksin and supporters of democracy.

The New Central Role of Media and Communicators

As the institutional bases of Network Thaksin in the parliament, political party, business groups, military and police were hammered apart, media acquired increased importance as the means of linking nodes within the network. In early 2007, the network launched PTV, a cable TV station. While pro-Thaksin parties returned to power over 2008–09, programming moved onto the government-owned NBT channel. After the fall of the Somchai government, the cable channel was relaunched as DTV in January 2009. Several other satellite stations were launched including Asia Update. Several hundred community radio stations were aligned with the network. In addition, there were several print publications and online sites.

A handful of popular speakers and commentators became important in this network, especially a trio nicknamed the "three musketeers." Veera (later Veerakarn) Musikapong had been a student activist in the 1970s, and later a Democrat Party MP, minister, and party secretary-general, who split from the party and joined up with Thaksin in the early 2000s. Jatuporn Phromphan had been a student activist who gained a reputation as an orator and became an early worker for the Thai Rak Thai Party. Nattawut Saikuea was a star student debater who became a TV personality, drafted into the network by Veera in 2005. These three had a key role hosting programs on the network's television stations, as well as speaking on public stages.

After 2006 their main focus was to bring Thaksin back home, using many strategies, including public demonstrations, television programs and petitions for amnesty.

The media outlets were also used to promote Thaksin and the Red Shirts as defenders of democracy and representatives of the grassroots in society. Several intellectual figures contributed to this task, including some that had earlier supported the Communist Party of Thailand and still had left-leaning ideas.

The network also used other methods of outreach. News, information and programming were distributed to community radio stations in the provinces. Academics and politicians organized "UDD schools" by circulating round the provinces holding two or three day events focusing on basic political understanding. This outreach extended to sympathetic groups formed amongst Thais living overseas in such places as Japan, the US and Australia.[18]

Remnants from the Military and Police

As noted above, the network that Thaksin had begun to build in the army was dispersed by systematic purges. However support for Thaksin was not entirely eradicated from the military and remained strong in the police. The press coined the term *thahan taengmo* "watermelon soldiers," meaning they wore a green uniform on the outside but were red in their hearts. They helped the network by providing political analysis and leaking news from within the military. Sometimes they ignored the official orders of their immediate superiors if such orders were against the interests of the Red Shirts.[19] Another set of soldiers no longer on active service helped with training guards for Red Shirt rallies, including a group that called itself the "King Tak Warriors" after the monarch who revived Siam following defeat by Burma in the late 18th century and who was overthrown by the founder of the Chakri dynasty. The press also coined the term *tamruat makhuethet*, "tomato police," red both outside and in, for officers who supported the Red Shirts.

The Changing Faces and Roles of Business

Most of the big business groups so prominent in the first version of Network Thaksin had distanced themselves from Thaksin by the time of the coup or soon after. There were, however, a handful that remained loyal, including Anant Asavabhokhin and Prayuth Mahakitsiri.

Anant Asavabhokhin, head of Land and Houses, one of the largest real estate companies, had been on the fringes of the political world since the early 1990s.[20] He was a classmate and close friend of Boonklee Plangsiri, a close aide and advisor to Thaksin. His Land

and Houses company was one of the major supporters of Voice TV, owned by the Shinawatra family.

Prayuth Mahakitsiri had interests stretching across steel, film, real estate, and a relationship with Nestle. He was a long-time friend of Thaksin, an early supporter of his political career, and often his golf partner. His son went into partnership with Thaksin's son in selling mobile phones, and became a deputy government spokesman during the Samak government. Prayuth supported Red Shirt rallies by supplying food.[21]

Many smaller but nevertheless prominent businessmen became active participants in the second version of Network Thaksin. They included owners of department stores, bus companies, fresh markets, and construction businesses. Some had profited from Thaksin's measure to assist domestic capital after the Asian financial crisis and wished to show their gratitude. Others were opposed to military intervention in politics. As mass politics became the mode of both Thaksin and his opposition, the roles of business supporters also changed. Where many businessmen had earlier limited their political involvement to donating money, they now became involved in organizing meetings and directly canvassing support. Here, three examples will be described.

Songkhram Kitloetpairoj from Samut Prakan was owner of the Imperial department store with branches in Samrong and Lat Phrao, and a former chairman of the Chamber of Commerce in Samut Prakan. During the economic crisis of 1997, Imperial Department store was deeply indebted but survived through debt restructuring under the government's Thai Asset Management scheme, and underwent a facelift in 2007. Songkhram was elected as MP in 2005 and 2007, becoming treasurer of Thaksin's party and a deputy minister of commerce in the Somchai cabinet. His younger brother was also on the party executive, and was barred from politics for five years after the party was dissolved, but his wife won the seat in 2011.

Songkhram was active as leader of the "Paknam group"[22] and led workers from Samut Prakan to join several Red Shirt rallies. His department store building in Samrong became a Red Shirt center, especially for taxi drivers. His department store in Lat Phrao housed the Red Shirt television stations (PTV and Asia Update), and many programs were shot inside the store. During the height of Red Shirt street campaigns, the Lat Phrao store functioned as the nerve centre of the mobilization. The fifth and sixth floors were full of small shops selling OTOP[23] products, including cosmetics and herbal medicine, and also Red Shirt souvenirs, hats, garments, belts, newspapers, magazines, and DVD speeches of red politicians.[24] At the time of the Bangkok floods in 2011, the store was a center for distributing goods donated through Red Shirt organizations. The car park was used by taxi drivers, who often turned on CDs of core Red Shirt speeches for passengers, talked to them about their political views, and relayed news about Red Shirt activities.[25] The department store was not only a commercial space but also a political space.

Phaiwong Techanarongran, owner of a resort called Bonanza Golf and Country Club in Nakhon Ratchasima, helped to organize Red Shirt activities after the 2006 coup.[26] He was both leader and main supporter of UDD in Los Angeles. He was chairman of the tabloid newspaper, *Bangkok Today*, and wrote columns under the name "Fighting Cock." During the first Thaksin government, one of his companies was contracted to install solar cells at government offices. He was also involved in a real estate project with the Wongsawat family.[27] After the 2011 election, Phaiwong was appointed advisor to the interior minister.

Phetcharawat Watthanapongsirikul, former owner of hotel and bus companies, became a leader of the "Love Chiang Mai 51 Group," and helped to make Chiang Mai a "capital city of the Red Shirts."[28]

The Red Shirt Movement in the Rural Northeast

Prior to the 2006 coup, Thaksin enjoyed strong support from the provinces, especially in the northeast and upper north, as shown by his election victories and the crowds that attended his upcountry tours. After the coup removed Thaksin, this support base was transformed into something more than electoral support through the Red Shirt movement.

Even though the core of the Red Shirts came from the countryside, the movement was not based on the economic grievances of the farming class, as had been the case with the Farmers Federation of Thailand in the 1970s, or the exclusion issues raised by the NGO-based Assembly of the Poor in the 1980s (Pinkaew 2013). The red movement was more complex, consisting of many groups of varying social and economic backgounds and with many political ideas.

Rural societies in developing countries all over the world have been undergoing rapid and deep transformation in the last part of the 20th century. In Thailand, especially in the northeast, Somchai Phatharathananunth (2012) described the development of a "post-peasant society" with agriculture becoming more commercialized, more rural migrants working in the cities or overseas, remittance flows transforming the local economy, and the coming of electricity and communications technology giving access to the wider world. These changes integrated rural societies with the urban economy.

In the northeast, cash crops such as cassava were increasingly grown under contract-farming arrangements with agri-business companies such as the CP group. The change in production relations led to changes in political structure and ideology. Farmers became more individualistic. The *kamnan* (subdistrict head) and village headmen lost much of their influence. Like entrepreneurs everywhere, farmers became interested in how the market worked and how it could be influenced. Villagers became less fearful of state power, and increasingly looked for assistance from national and local politicians rather than bureaucrats. They had their own views on politics, and had access to news and information.

These basic economic and political changes prepared the way for the emergence of the Red Shirts. The personality and policies of Thaksin provided the impetus. In his first term, Thaksin put in place the Universal Health Care scheme, several windows of micro-credit, and some agricultural price subsidies, especially for rice. These policies were perceived to have an impact on ordinary people's lives far beyond anything experienced under previous governments (Naruemon and McCargo 2013). Thaksin also presented himself as a leader of the ordinary people, responsive to their demands, unlike any predecessor. Many who later came to join the Red Shirts explained that they felt grateful to Thaksin for his policies and for the sense of empowerment he gave them.[29]

As a result, when Thaksin was toppled by coup in 2006, many villagers in the north, northeast and central regions saw this as wrong and came out to join demonstrations.[30] After the clashes with the security forces at Sanam Luang, Victory Monument and Dindaeng junction in Bangkok in April–May 2010, many became even more opposed to state power and more sympathetic to Thaksin.

Phruek Thaothawin (2010) showed that villagers' political sophistication advanced election by election. Vote buying declined in effectiveness, as people increasingly paid attention to the policies on offer. Electors became increasingly aware of the power of the vote and their ability to use it to bring about improvement in their own lives. Loyalty to Thaksin was less and less about Thaksin himself and more and more an expression of the villagers' wish to protect their newly gained and understood power.

Pinkaew Laungaramsri (2013) found that the Red Shirt movement reflected the development of democratic attitudes in rural Thailand. Decentralization, electoral politics, as well as economic and political changes in the Thai countryside have contributed to a political awakening and new enthusiasm for political participation. Villagers, vendors and market traders in Chiang Mai and other centres in the north became involved in campaigns to oppose the coup and protect democracy. The identity of the Red Shirts did not emerge immediately but was shaped gradually over the five years after the 2006 coup (Nopphon 2013).

In summary several studies have described how ordinary villagers and urban groups from taxi drivers to market vendors were transformed into political activists, creating new organizations and networks among themselves in a way that had not been seen in earlier social movements.

Another side of the Red Shirts: Kwanchai Phraiphana

> These people [chasing Thaksin away] must be burnt, using used car tires, kill them, go to surround their houses or shops. (Kwanchai Phraiphana, Khluen Muanchon Samphan Radio, June 2006)[31]

Kwanchai Phraiphana and a community radio station in Udon Thani fiercely supported Thaksin. Kwanchai mobilized people to break up PAD's attempt to stage a rally in the province. He sent out application forms for people to become members of the "Love Udon Thani People's Forum." He organized parties to travel to Bangkok, Laos and Dubai to meet and give moral support to Thaksin.

Kwanchai was a native of Suphanburi. After completing elementary education, he traveled around to seek his fortune. He worked as a comedian with a country music band, and was in the troupe of a famous singer Sayan Sanya when he was at the height of his career. Later he ran a country music program on a popular Udon Thani radio station, playing Sayan Sanya songs interspersed with advertising. When the PAD started their demonstrations against Thaksin in 2005, he gave support to Thaksin through the radio and helped to found the Love Udon Thani People's Forum.

Kwanchai moved closely with the MPs, local politicians, senior bureaucrats and police, and business figures in Udon. Through his morning-time radio show, he helped to construct Udon as a "capital" of the Red Shirts by persistently attacking and issuing threats against businessmen and officials who openly opposed Thaksin. An online newspaper reported that he incited people to surround the house and gold shop of the PAD leader in the town.[32] When PAD attempted to hold a rally in the province, Kwanchai and others led a group of some thousand people to break up the rally, resulting in 22 people being injured, two seriously. On other occasions he led groups to blockade an attempt by two PAD leaders to hold an anti-Thaksin rally in Udon,[33] and an attempt by Udon PAD leaders to hold a press conference in Bangkok. After the 2006 coup he lay low in Laos for a time, before returning to help organize pro-Thaksin demonstrations in Bangkok. He joined the Red Shirt demonstrations against the Abhisit government[34] both in April 2009 and in April–May 2010.[35]

Like other local Red Shirt leaders, Kwanchai claimed to have a special relationship with Thaksin: he could talk to Thaksin directly on the phone, or ring his secretary or relatives. Such claims enhanced Kwanchai's image in the locality, but also provoked opposition. Kwanchai also angered people by claiming that he had personally provided 20 million baht to buy land and build a center for the Love Udon Thani People's Forum whereas others claimed the money had come from a fund-raising dinner.[36] Local groups attacked Kwanchai over this and other issues on online media.[37]

Some time after the 2006 coup, certain villages in the northeast declared themselves as "Red Shirt villages." The movement gathered momentum over 2010–11, and by June 2011 there were reported to be over 320 such villages in the provinces of Udon Thani and Khon Kaen alone.[38] Kwanchai disagreed with the idea of Red Shirt villages on grounds that the reputation of the Red Shirts would be damaged by association with drugs and other illegal activities in these villages. Kwanchai was increasingly in conflict with other Red Shirt groups in the province, including his earlier supporters.

After the Yingluck government was installed in July 2011, the Red Shirts adopted a more conciliatory stance. On the occasion of the King's birthday in December 2011, a leading Red Shirt composed a song for the King, and several Red Shirt leaders made a recording at the Asia Update studios in Imperial Lat Phrao, with Thaksin joining the singing by phone.[39] Kwanchai joined this trend, leading a group of 999 Red Shirts from 20 provinces entering the monkhood to make merit for the King's seventh cycle. Kwanchai announced on this occasion, "I as a royally sponsored monk will adhere to the *thamma* and pray for His Majesty every day."[40] Tensions returned, however, when opponents began street demonstrations in Bangkok in October 2013 aimed at bringing down the Yingluck government. On January 23, 2014, Kwanchai Praipana was shot and injured in the shoulder and leg. A day earlier, he had criticized an official who claimed the "men in black" that provoked violence during the 2010 protests were foreign militia, and had offered a reward of 500,000 baht (about US$17,000) for anyone who could capture Suthep Thaugsuban, the leader of the anti-Yingluck street protests.

Conclusion

The first version of Network Thaksin developed in the late 1990s and early 2000s. Its primary bases were in business, the army and police, and among provincial politicians. In this respect, it was similar to the networks constructed by Thai civilian political leaders over the previous 20 to 30 years. Big businessmen were unusually prominent in the network, and Thaksin also had a base of mass electoral support, but initially these factors did not seem to make this network fundamentally different from earlier models.

From 2005, Thaksin's opponents set out to tear this network apart, with some success. However, Network Thaksin did not disappear but was reshaped and revived. This came about in part because the destruction of the three main bases was far from complete. Many provincial politicians and some business figures stayed openly loyal to Thaksin, and circles of covert support remained in the uniformed forces. But the survival of the network was principally due to the survival of the mass base, and a greater level of participation from many different groups and interests. As a result the second version of the network was more complex and different in shape. The first version can be drawn as a pyramid, but the second is a web.

After the coup, Thaksin took refuge abroad. Thaksin's network power was no longer constructed by Thaksin alone, but by many groups with many interests and ideologies. The development of the network was not systematic but a gradual adaptation to changed political circumstances.

The new network was shaped by the unprecedented level of mass involvement in Thai politics. To a large extent, modern media and communications formed the platform of the revived network and made possible involvement by many groups with different concerns including defense of democracy, social justice, and the interests of regions that had felt neglected by the over-centralized Thai state.

A major part of this rural mass participation was the Red Shirt contingent from the rural upper north and northeast. Their politicization was a function of the social and economic changes of the past 30 years which had moved them away from subsistence agriculture and into contract farming, cash cropping, and migrant labor. Villagers had become more individualistic, less susceptible to control by village heads and bureaucrats, and more aware of what they could gain through electoral politics at the local and national level.

The objectives of the network were also more varied. A primary objective was to defend the interests of Thaksin himself, but other objectives included contesting the authority of those who made the 2006 coup, and advancing the cause of democracy. Strategies were also more varied: they included contesting elections to win state power, but also organizing street demonstrations, and spreading political awareness. Different participants had differing opinions over strategy, particularly on the issue of violence. Because of the variety of participants, objectives, and strategies, there were constant disagreements among different factions of the network.

The campaign to overthrow this network was concerted and prolonged. Two prime ministers and several ministers were removed by judicial process; over 200 MPs were banned from politics for five years; the results of four elections were invalidated; and demonstrations occupied the streets of the capital for many months. The second coup, which came in 2014, differed significantly from other coups in the past 40 years. The coup-makers were more aggressive, kept power in their own hands, retained martial law for many months, brooked almost no expression of dissent or opposition, and hand-picked bodies to write a new constitution and many other reforms. While the coup brought back the familiar structure of oligarchic power (military, business, bureaucracy), the new constitution and other reforms were designed to protect this structure for the long term.

While the downfall of Thaksin can be explained in part in personal terms, the campaign to overthrow his network and resurrect the old structure of power requires a broader form of explanation.

Thaksin's second network had gone beyond the bounds of flexible oligarchy.

Network Thaksin represented a rising new form of oligarchy in Thailand, based on wealth rapidly accumulated in telecommunication businesses and stock market dealings, and a popular base that delivered two landslide election victories. Moreover, because Thaksin's oligarchy had democratic legitimation, it was not responsive to other elements of the "flexible oligarchy" of the past. In fact, it was their real enemy.

The Siamese-twin coups of 2006 and 2014 were made by the same military group, backed by the same political alliance, and with the same political target, namely destruction of Network Thaksin. This political alliance wishes to turn Thailand back into an older type of oligarchy with a formal pyramid topped by the rich few in a revitalized form designed for the complex, open and globalized Thailand of today. Achieving this plan, however, means weakening all democratic institutions and widening the inequalities of wealth, power and privilege. It remains to be seen whether the outdated formula of military power and bureaucratic rule can be sustained for long.

Notes

1. Somchai Wongsawat (prime minister September–December 2008) is Thaksin's brother-in-law. Yingluck Shinawatra (August 2011 to May 2014) is his younger sister. Samak Sundaravej (January–September 2008) told an interviewer, "Someone asked me: 'Are you the nominee of Thaksin?' I said what's wrong with this word, 'nominee?' What's wrong with this word?" See Hannah Beech, "Thailand's Prime Minister Speaks", Time Magazine, May 5, 2008, available at http:www.times.com/time/world/article/0,8599,1737674,00,html#ixzz2d3hgevj7 [accessed Aug. 26, 2013].

2. The government led by General Chatichai Choonhawan (1989–91) had drawn support from local influential politicians, such as Narong Wongwan, Montri Pongpanich, Banharn Silapa-archa, Suwat Lipatapanlop and new-generation businessmen such as Pairoj Piampongsan, but all of these politicians went on to support successive governments under Chuan Leekpai (1992–95, 1997–2001), Banharn Silapa-archa (1995–96) and General Chavalit Yongchaiyudh (1996–97).

3. *Bangkok Post*, July 15, 1998.

4. Thaksin Shinawatra's address to the Annual General Meeting of the Thai Rak Thai Party, Thammasat University, Rangsit, Mar. 26, 2000.

5. Thaksin Shinawatra's address to the Annual General Meeting of the Thai Rak Thai Party, Thammasat University, Rangsit, Apr. 22, 2001.

6. The government interfered in the debt restructuring, which angered foreign creditors, including representatives from the International Finance Corporation (IFC), linked to the World Bank. The US ambassador was also unhappy with this method. *The Economist*, June 21, 2003.

7. In November 2001 Grammy Entertainment began collecting fees for intellectual property rights on songs broadcast in any entertainment complex. This announcement caused conflict between Grammy and its rival firms, but the commerce minister refused to intervene.

8. *Phujatkan*, Oct. 1, 2001; *Phim Thai*, Oct. 12, 2002; *Phim Thai*, Aug. 27, 2003.

9. Wassana Nanuam, "Defense Gets B 3bn after King's Request," *Bangkok Post*, July 20, 2003.

10. *Phim Thai*, Oct. 12, 2002.

11. Wassana Nanuam, "Defense Gets B 3bn after King's Request," *Bangkok Post*, July 20, 2003.

12. *The Nation*, Aug. 30, 2000.

13. Sudarat Keyuraphan told a newspaper that Thaksin rang Samak directly to confirm the agreement that Samak would be the party leader; cited in *The Nation*, Aug. 1, 2007.

14. Wassana Nanuam, "Army has no Role in Politics," *Bangkok Post*, Sept. 20, 2007.

15. Signs of non-cooperation had appeared earlier. On June 1, Samak announced that he would move the protesters by force. A few days after this Anupong said "I am not the government's soldier. The army belongs to the Thai people. I could not function as a personal soldier of anyone.... I am always on the side of the people." Cited in *Bangkok Post*, June 12, 2008.

16. *The Nation*, Sept. 3, 2008.

17. *Krungthep Thurakit*, Feb. 21, 2010.

18. Interviews with many Thai restaurant owners in Tokyo, Kobe, Kyoto and Osaka in Japan in Feb.–June 2010.

19. Interview with a general in the Supreme Command, Dec. 11, 2011.

20. "Anant fueang yuk Thaksin poet khwam samphan thai rak thai" [Anant's Rise in Thaksin Era Reveals Relations with Thai Rak Thai], *Phujatkan rai sapda*, Dec. 22, 2005, available at http://www.manager.co.th/mgrWeekly/viewNews.aspx?newsID=9480000175419 [accessed Mar. 29, 2015].

21. William Barnes, "Sifting through Thailand's Ashes," *Asia Times*, May 22, 2010. Available at http://www.atimes.com/atimes/Southeast Asia/LE22Ae01.html.

22. The rivermouth (*paknam*) of the Chao Phraya is in Samut Prakan province.

23. One Tambon (village) One Product, name of a scheme for promoting local products that the first Thaksin government adapted from Japan.

24. Surveyed by author, Jan. 10, 2012.

25. Surveyed by author, Feb. 4, 2012.

26. "Daeng kwa 5 muen kon hae ruam konsoet thi bonanza khao yai Thaksin jo phon in 2 thum" [More than 50,000 Reds Flock to Concert at Bonanza, Khaoyai; Thaksin Phone-in 8 pm], Matichon Online, available at http://www.matichon.co.th/newsdetail.php?Newsid=1330166157&grpid=02&catid=2.

27. "Suea daeng L.A. dai he phaiwong techanarong dai rap pen thi phrueksa mo to 1" [Red Shirts LA Cheer Phaiwong Techanarong as Advisor to Interior Minister], available at http://www.oknation.net/blog/Ilusions/2011/09/06/entry-1.

28. Interview with a NGO leader in Chiang Mai, Feb. 5, 2012.

29. Interview Somchai Phatharathananunth, Apr. 25, 2012.

30. Interview with villagers at the demonstration at Ratprasong junction and in front of the Siam Center, Bangkok, Apr. 16–19, 2010; interview with Phruek Thaothawin, Apr. 24, 2012; interview with an NGO leader, Chiang Mai.

31. http://www.udon108.com/board/index.php?topic=2078.Msg47250 [accessed Nov. 1, 2010].

32. "Phlik pum thoi Kwanchai Phraphana kaen lai khon phantamit udon" [Push the Ejector Button: Kwanchai Phraphana, Putting the Udon PAD to Flight], available at http:www.manager.co.th/politics/ViewNews.aspx?NewsID=9510000087450 [accessed Nov. 1, 2010].

33. "Poet pum kwanchai phraiphana" [Exposing Kwanchai Phraiphana], available at http://politics.spiceday.com/redirect.php?tid=3571&goto=lastpost&sid=GVCC7 [accessed Nov. 1, 2010].

34. Abhisit Vejjajiva, leader of the Democrat Party, became prime minister in December 2008 after the pro-Thaksin government was felled by the courts. He was defeated at elections in July 2011.

35. "Jap phutongha kokan jalajon" [Arrest of Suspects Causing Riots], ASTV Manager Online, May 21, 2010, available at http://www.tnews.co.th/html/read.php?hot_id=12120 [accessed Jan. 4, 2011].

36. Television station Asia Update, Oct. 22, 2009.

37. "Chaloem ya suek daeng da phra kwanchai" [Chalerm Stops the War between Kwanchai and Other Reds], *Khom Chat Luek*, Jan. 10, 2012.

38. Jason Szep and Ambika Ahuja, "Defiance in Thailand's 'Red Shirt Villages'," Reuters, June 7, 2011, available at http://www.reuters.com/article/2011/06/07/us-thailandelection-idUSTRE75614T20110607.

39. "Thaksin rong phlaeng rachan ong phumiphon" [Thaksin Sings 'Rachan Ong Bhumibol'], *Matichon*, Dec. 9, 2011.
40. Ibid.

References

Hewison, Kevin. 2004. "Crafting Thailand's New Social Contract." *Pacific Review* 17, 4: 503–22.

McCargo, Duncan and Ukrist Pathmanand. 2005. *The Thaksinization of Thailand*. Copenhagen: Nordic Institute of Asian Studies.

McCargo, Duncan. 2005. "Network Monarchy and Legitimacy Crises in Thailand." *Pacific Review* 18, 4: 499–519.

_____. ed. 2002. *Reforming Thai Politics*. Copenhagen: NIAS.

Naruemon Thabchumpon and Duncan McCargo. 2013. "Urbanized Villagers in the 2010 Thai Redshirt Protests: Not Just Poor Farmers?" *Asian Survey* 51, 6: 993–1018.

Nopphon Achamat. 2013. "Kan doen thang khong mae kha suea daeng: jak talat su kanmueang bon thong thanon" [The Journey of Red Shirt Vendors from Markets to Street Politics]. In *Becoming Red: Kamnoet lae phatthanakan suea daeng nai Chiang Mai* [Birth and Development of the Red Shirt Movement in Chiang Mai], ed. Pinkaew Laungaramsri. Chiang Mai: Chiang Mai University, pp. 67–96.

Pasuk Phongpaichit and Chris Baker, ed. 2008. *Thai Capital after the 1997 Crisis*. Chiang Mai: Silkworm Books.

_____. 2009. *Thaksin*. 2nd ed., Chiang Mai: Silkworm Books.

Phruek Thaothawin. 2010. "Kabuankan suea daeng kanmueang thongthin lae prachathippatai" [The Redshirt Movement, Local Politics, and Democracy]. *Fa Dieo Kan* [Same Sky] 8, 2 (Oct.–Dec.): 108–31.

Pinkaew Laungaramsri. 2013. "Mue phuak khao dai klai pen 'suea daeng': kan mueang muanchon ruam samai nai jangwat chiang mai" [When They Become 'Red Shirts': Contemporary Mass Politics in Chiang Mai]. In *Becoming Red: Kamnoet lae phatthanakan suea daeng nai Chiang Mai* [Birth and Development of the Red Shirt Movement in Chiang Mai], ed. Pinkaew Laungaramsri. Chiang Mai: Chiang Mai University, pp. 33–66.

Somchai Phatharathananunth. 2012. "The Politics of Postpeasant Society: The Emergence of the Rural Red Shirts in Northeast Thailand." Unpublished paper.

Thitinan Pongsudhirak. 2003. "Thailand: Democratic Authoritarianism." In *Southeast Asian Affairs 2003*. Singapore: Institute of Southeast Asian Studies.

9

Tax Reform for a More Equal Society

Moderate income inequality is acceptable and can serve as an incentive for people to work harder with benefits for an economy. But extreme inequality is unjust and can lead to social problems (Greenspan 2007). The methods and means of taxation may either contribute to inequality, or be designed to promote better distribution of income and wealth. This chapter reviews four areas where reforms of the tax system can help to reduce inequality in Thailand. The four areas are: tax incentives for investment promotion, exemptions and allowances on personal income tax, negative income tax, and wealth taxes.

Reform of Investment Promotion

Past development has created an unbalanced economy with ever-increasing dependence on exports. Policy has focused on attracting foreign investment especially for industry, and has neglected the development of small and medium enterprises. Research by the National Economic and Social Development Board (NESDB 2011) found that large enterprises have been able to bias policy for the benefit of capital rather than labor, with the result that the share of earned income (wages and salaries) in national income is only around 40 per cent while unearned income (profits, interests and rent) take 60 per cent. Over the past decade, the share of earned income has even declined (see Figure 9.1). The taxation system further exacerbates inequality as there is a strict system for taxing wages and salaries while the returns to capital are taxed at a lower level as a result of loopholes in the taxation laws which facilitate evasion (NESDB 2011).

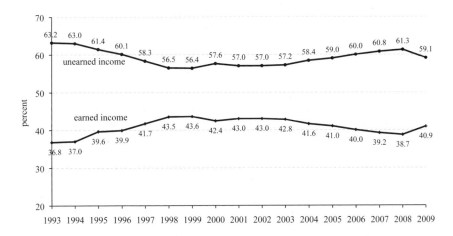

Figure 9.1 Shares of Earned and Unearned Income in Total National Income, 1993–2009

Source: NESDB (2011: 63).

Promotion of foreign investment, particularly for industry, uses exemptions, reductions and holidays on corporate taxation and import dues for machinery and inputs. This policy can be counted a success, but has created several problems, especially in favoring large-scale enterprises, creating spatial concentration, reducing the revenue of government by over 300 billion baht a year (more than the total return from personal income tax), and promoting industries without any clear strategy.

Moreover investment promotion and investment prevention are two sides of the same coin, as giving favors to some also creates burdens for others. To moderate this injustice, the government should limit promotion to individual cases that conform to the nation's development strategy and are of special importance.

Reform of investment promotion has gained support among officials and academics. For instance, Somphong Wanapha, former secretary-general of the Board of Investment (BOI), said, "Tax concessions granted by BOI to attract investment are only one kind of tool, and we should not fall into this trap because under globalization taxation measures are disappearing" (*Than Sethakit*, Dec. 4–7, 2011). Similarly Sathit Rangsiri stated while he was director-general of the Revenue Department,

> Why do we have to reduce taxes for BOI but not for Thais? Why not for the whole country? Why only support some people? We have strayed to the point where anyone building a building or expanding a business to reduce pollution can deduct the whole construction expense from tax…. It's equivalent to having the Revenue Department build the building for you. Do we have to go this extent? Does it increase Thailand's GDP? Do the Thai profit by a single baht? He'd have to build the building anyway, right? Why are we giving this away?
>
> BOI promotion began from the time of Field Marshals Sarit and Phibun. At that time, there were walls between countries, tax barriers. Now these have disappeared. We should not just be letting [foreign investors] in, but we should be promoting Thais to invest overseas too. Has that been done? The market is not 60 million but 600 million. Has the thinking changed yet? No…. If there was no BOI, and corporate tax was 15 per cent for the whole country, would we be happier? Would you like that, or would you like to stay as is, just benefiting a few companies? (Seminar on "Tax reform for entering the AEC," Nov. 9, 2012)

However, reforming investment promotion has many limitations and difficulties. Teerana Bhongmakapat (2006) once noted, "Many economists don't like the BOI's tax incentives for industrial entrepreneurs. But the policy proposals that economists want have not been accepted by politicians or governments for over two decades."

Reforming Personal Income Tax Exemptions and Allowances

In theory personal income tax is a direct tax based on ability to pay as measured by income. In estimating the ability to pay, many countries take into account family size and various expenses, and allow reductions and exemptions accordingly. As a result, income tax is generally accepted as fair all over the world. However the exemptions and reductions reduce the government's income.

In Thailand, the system is not designed to be fair. The system facilitates tax evasion by the rich and thus contradicts the principles of fair taxation and ability to pay. Many of the exemptions and allowances result in low-income people subsidizing the high-income ones.

Figure 9.2 and Table 9.1 show the average amount claimed as various kinds of allowance by tax-payers in different income brackets. The data show that the higher the income, the greater is the amount claimed in allowances and exemptions.

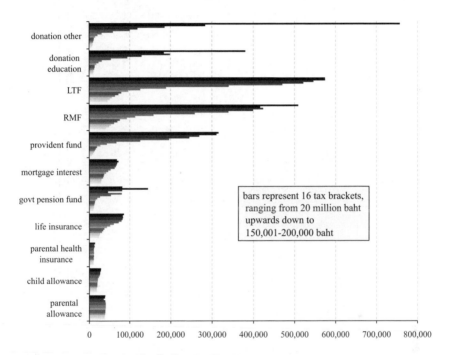

Figure 9.2 Usage of Income Tax Allowances by Income Level, 2008

Note: 2008 means 2008 tax year; unit is baht, average per head
Source: Ministry of Finance.

If we use one million baht net income per year as a dividing line between low-income and high-income, then there are certain allowances where the usage between low-income and high-income tax-payers is not significantly different. These are the parental allowance, child allowance, and allowance for parental medical insurance. In the case of allowances for life insurance, the government pension fund, and mortgage interest, the high-income tax-payers make more claims than low-income. And in the case of the Retirement Mutual Fund (RMF), Long-term Equity Fund (LTF), provident fund, donations

Table 9.1 Usage of Income Tax Allowances by Income Level, 2008

Net annual income level	Same usage by low and high income			More usage by high-income			Much more usage by high-income				
	Parental allowance	Child allowance	Parental health insurance	Life insurance fund	Government pension	Mortgage interest	Provident fund	Retirement Mutual Fund	Long-term Equity Fund	Donations for education	Other donations
150,001–200,000	39,382	19,398	10,544	21,931	8,434	28,305	6,374	35,909	41,531	8,984	6,081
200,001–250,000	38,713	19,083	10,775	23,702	9,680	28,635	7,958	41,600	44,717	10,001	7,227
250,001–300,000	38,122	18,375	10,249	25,021	10,748	29,147	9,624	48,956	50,262	10,829	8,200
300,001–350,000	38,302	18,181	10,534	26,205	11,471	29,851	11,398	53,036	55,250	10,436	8,318
350,001–400,000	38,870	19,330	10,919	31,140	11,904	33,798	13,686	60,957	63,198	12,468	9,776
400,001–450,000	39,035	19,616	10,543	34,001	12,778	35,150	16,100	68,944	71,630	13,340	10,874
450,001–500,000	39,312	19,682	11,352	36,843	13,763	36,604	19,020	75,068	78,679	13,589	11,654
500,001–750,000	39,749	20,535	10,908	43,252	15,205	41,135	27,180	92,580	96,375	17,518	15,059
750,001–1,000,000	40,013	20,759	11,548	50,885	19,171	46,339	43,144	113,706	126,117	22,999	20,375
1,000,001–2,000,000	39,992	21,308	11,054	59,738	26,236	52,181	66,631	158,576	189,290	30,887	30,625
2,000,001–4,000,000	40,078	23,045	10,756	72,121	52,674	61,839	126,184	258,467	340,632	53,129	58,216
4,000,001–6,000,000	39,751	25,200	11,567	78,997	79,646	65,002	196,724	339,723	470,216	93,833	100,375
6,000,001–8,000,000	38,846	26,480	12,912	81,595	45,765	66,857	245,299	399,483	521,674	129,554	119,522
8,000,001–10,000,000	35,310	26,737	12,102	83,028	80,649	68,265	269,236	423,824	546,290	198,772	185,938
10,000,001–20,000,000	38,321	28,216	14,000	82,082	144,761	71,530	310,887	416,380	574,634	183,873	283,946
20,000,001 up	39,091	28,654	0	85,186	81,082	67,601	315,941	509,050	574,231	380,907	756,561

Note: 2008 means 2008 tax year; unit is baht, average per head

Source: Author's calculations from Ministry of Finance data.

for education, and other donations, the difference between low-income and high-income is very marked.

This above analysis is based on the amount of allowance claimed. If we analyze by the amount of tax reduction given—which is equivalent to a government subsidy—the extent to which the system favors those of high income is even more marked. Those with net income of 150,000–200,000 baht get an average tax reduction (that is, subsidy) of 7,380 baht, rising to 133,895 per head for those with net income over 2 million baht (Figure 9.3). The system is clearly regressive.

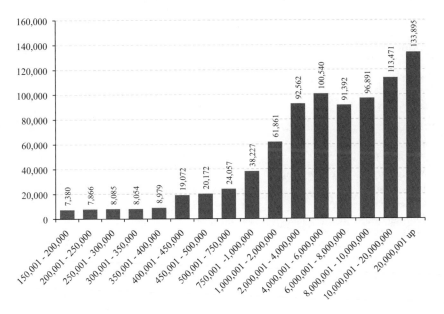

Figure 9.3 Reduction of Tax Liability through Allowances, 2008

Note: 2008 means 2008 tax year; unit is baht, average per head
Source: Author's calculation from Ministry of Finance data.

A simple reform would be to put a cap on the total amount of allowances claimable, perhaps at the level of 700,000 baht. Certain allowances should perhaps be withdrawn altogether. The LTFs are mutual funds aimed at promoting long-term investment in the stock market. Tax-payers who invest in these funds can claim up to 500,000 baht a year as allowance. Nualnoi Treerat (2013) argued that the allowance should be cancelled as, "No government in the world uses tax measures to support people playing the stock market. This measure should be used only during a stock market slump, not when the market is active, because it takes everyone's money to give to the rich."

Negative Income Tax

Over the past decade, state social security has increased and will continue to do so in the future. The government will eventually need to increase taxes as a result. The government constantly faces a problem of ensuring that social security reaches the intended recipients because it lacks the data to identify the poor. As a result a large part of social security goes to people who are not poor (Table 9.2).

Table 9.2 Access to Government Services Classified by Poverty Status, 2008

Service	Percentage		
	not poor	poor	total
Education loans	99.8	0.2	100.0
People's Bank	97.9	2.1	100.0
Village and community funds	91.2	8.8	100.0
Education grants	90.9	9.1	100.0
Other grants	89.2	10.8	100.0
Old-age pension	80.4	19.6	100.0
Disabled allowance	78.9	21.1	100.0

Source: Surajit Laksanasut et al. (2010: 52), using data from NESDB (2008).

A study by Jansen and Khannabha (2009) concluded that Thai fiscal policy did not contribute to reducing poverty or inequality because the amount involved is small and the targeting inefficient.

One way to overcome the problem of targeting is to use a negative income tax, a scheme first proposed by Milton Friedman in 1962. Friedman suggested that the government should set a guaranteed minimum income and pay subsidies to those whose income fell below that level. He argued that this system would cause less distortion to the free market than other kinds of transfer.

Systems of personal income tax usually allow citizens to deduct expenses and allowances from their gross income to arrive at the taxable net income, on grounds that the government should not levy tax on income needed for the basic necessities of living. But those whose income falls below the minimum amount qualifying for taxation do not benefit under this system. A negative income tax overcomes this problem by paying a subsidy to those whose income is below this minimum cut-off point. A negative income tax is a combination of taxation and social security.

Since 1975, the US has adopted this system under the title of the Earned Income Tax Credit. Citizens apply using the standard income tax form. The scheme avoids the common criticism that welfare payments discourage people from seeking work, and the credit is only available to those who work and have an income. As a result, the US scheme has been copied by other countries including Britain, Canada, Ireland, New Zealand, Australia, Singapore, Sweden, Israel and South Korea.

Negative Income Tax for Thailand

This section outlines a scheme of negative income tax proposed for Thailand under the title *ngoen on kae jon khon khayan* "Transfer for the assiduous poor." Under the scheme, all aged 15 and above would file an income tax form, and those whose income falls below a poverty line would qualify for a subsidy. In 2012, the poverty line set by NESDB was 30,000 baht per year, and 8.4 million people fell below this line. These are the target group for the scheme.

The subsidy is set as follows, through three stages. First, anyone with a gross income below 30,000 baht a year qualifies for a subsidy amounting to 20 per cent of earned income. Second, when the gross income is between 30,000 and 80,000 baht, the subsidy of 6,000 is reduced by 12 per cent of the income earned in excess of 30,000 baht (so for an income of 40,000 baht the subsidy is 6,000 − [0.12* (40,000 − 30,000)] = 4,800). Third, with an above 80,000 baht income, no subsidy is paid.

At each stage, the person is encouraged to work and seek more income as that will increase the net income. The rate of subsidy varies like climbing and descending a hill. At the beginning of the ascent, the hill is steep, that is the subsidy rate is high to incentivize the person to be assiduous. On the downslope, the subsidy gradually declines as income increases to encourage the person to work, and finally stops altogether (Figure 9.4).

The scheme is relatively economical compared to social security and populist schemes (such as the first car scheme which cost 90 billion baht in one year). The estimated budget cost is around 56 billion

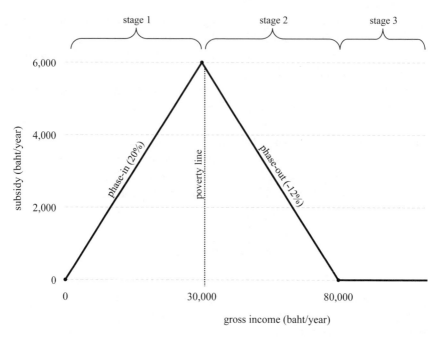

Figure 9.4   Proposal for a Negative Income Tax for Thailand

baht a year, and will reduce the number below the poverty line by an estimated 1.6 million persons.

The scheme has many advantages. Through the income tax application, it provides data on the poor that can be used for other programs and contexts. It puts money in the pockets of the right people, by accurately identifying the poor, and prevents subsidy of those not qualified. It reduces inequality without prejudicing economic growth, as the scheme does not discourage people from working and seeking higher incomes, unlike other schemes such as unemployment benefit. It has low operating costs, unlike social security schemes in which money is disbursed through the Thai bureaucratic system which may be slow and onerous. It does not distort the market mechanism as the subsidies are provided through cash payments, not through adjustment of prices as in schemes to subsidize farm prices or reduce the cost of fuels and household goods. People prefer cash payments to price-manipulation schemes as they have a choice on how the cash is used. It will increase the tax base by encouraging informal workers, who constitute 62 per cent of all labor (NESDB 2011), to enter the tax system in order to qualify for the subsidy, allowing the government to levy income tax when their incomes rise. It can serve as a substitute for welfare schemes that are badly targeted, hence increasing efficiency and reducing corruption in use of the budget.

Wealth Taxes

Under globalization, income tax schemes all over the world have become less progressive. Besides, income tax is not an effective instrument for combating inequality in countries with a high proportion of informal labor. As such, wealth taxes have a role to play in reducing inequality.

Wealth taxes are levied on the ownership, transfer or change of assets. They are the oldest kind of tax in the English-speaking world. Lynn (1967) traced a "wealth tax cycle" through history. In Europe, taxes were first levied on land, then extended to almost every kind of personal property, and then gradually thinned down until only a land tax remained. Similarly, in the first two centuries of the US, taxes were levied on all kinds of private property including real estate, tangible assets and intangible assets (Netzer 1966), but subsequently the types of property taxed were gradually thinned down on grounds of the difficulty and inefficiency of collection. Most states today levy no property taxes except on real estate (Li 2006).

In the past two decades, as a result of financial decentralization and democratization, local governments in many countries have levied taxes on property, which now are at an average of 2.1 per cent of GDP in developed countries as a whole. In the developing countries, however, the rate is much lower at 0.6 per cent of GDP (USAID 2009a: 1; Bahl 2009: 4). In Thailand wealth taxes contribute only 0.2 per cent of GDP.

Under globalization the tax structure has shifted from direct taxes on income to indirect taxes on consumption. This shift increases inequality as consumption taxes tend to be regressive, and weigh heavier on those of lower income. Wealth taxes offer an opportunity to reverse this trend.

USAID (2009b: 22) observed that "if property ownership is concentrated in the higher income classes...the distribution of tax burdens for a property transfer tax will be progressive." Wealth taxes are thus appropriate for Thailand. The ownership of land is very concentrated (see Chapter 2), and the ownership of assets in general is rather concentrated compared to other countries in Asia (Davies et al. 2008). Land ownership is positively correlated with income. In 2009, around two-thirds of all households in the top income quintile owned at least 20 rai of land, while in the bottom income quintile, 70 per cent owned less than 20 rai.

In Thailand, tax has been levied on land and buildings since 1932, and local development taxes have been raised by local government since 1965, but these taxes are outdated and defective. For example, the local development tax is regressive, and the annual amount raised is small, around 20 billion baht or 1 per cent of total government revenue.

Property taxes are thus a good option for achieving the twin aims of increasing government revenue and reducing inequality. Several other countries have adopted this strategy. Here, four examples will be presented.

South Korea

Around 30 years ago, real estate prices increased sharply with severe impact on income distribution and security (Kim 2005). In addition, rising inequality became a concern after the financial crisis in 1997 (Jones 2009). The government responded by imposing wealth taxes which by 2006 delivered revenue equivalent to 3.5 per cent of GDP, compared to an OECD average of 2.1 per cent, and 13.2 per cent of total government revenue, compared to an OECD average of 5.7 per cent (Jones 2009).

The chief wealth taxes in Korea are property transaction taxes that alone deliver revenue equivalent to 2.4 per cent of GDP. These include an acquisition tax, raised by local government bodies on purchases of real estate, vehicles, planes and other capital goods; a registration tax levied on changes of registered ownership and other registered transactions; and a capital gains tax levied by the central government on capital gains at transfers of high-end real estate (value of around 18 million baht upwards), at a progressive rate based on both the asset value and the length of ownership (to discourage speculation).[2]

Other wealth taxes in Korea are recurrent property taxes of two kinds. Local government bodies raise a property tax based on value and usage of the property at a graduated rate ranging from 0.15 to 0.5 per cent. This tax delivers revenue equivalent to 0.5 per cent of GDP (Jones 2009). The central government since 2005 collects a house tax on properties worth over 600 million won (around 12 million baht) with a very progressive structure ranging from 1 to 3 per cent (Kim 2008).

Taiwan

Taiwan's success with property taxes has been praised as a contribution to both economic development and social justice (Tsui 2006). These taxes have been designed both to raise revenue and to promote income distribution.

Taiwan has a land value tax, house tax and a land value increment tax which is a capital gains tax on land transfers. The land value increment tax is intended to reclaim for the government that portion of the rise in property prices that results from the government's investments in infrastructure. The principle behind this tax has been inscribed in Taiwan's constitution (Tsui 2006). The tax takes a share of the windfall gains from property inflation, is used to finance the creation of public goods, and also helps to limit property speculation (Case 1994; Guevara 1997; Pugh 1997).

The land tax, levied only in urban areas, is based on the assessed value of land at a progressive structure from 1 to 5.5 per cent. The land value increment tax is levied on the difference between the sale price and the earlier purchase price. If the price has doubled, the rate is 20 per cent of the capital gain, and if tripled the rate is 40 per cent of the capital gain plus 50 per cent of the earlier purchase price.

Japan

In the bubble economy between 1985 and 1990, urban land prices in Japan tripled on average, increasing the gap between those with landed property and those without, and spawning resentment at the injustice. As the tax burden on land was low, land was a popular investment resulting in price inflation and suboptimal usage of land (Ishi 2001).

In 1992, Japan reformed both its land tax and capital gains tax on land transfers with the aim of making the tax system fairer, discouraging land speculation, and inducing more efficient use of land (Ministry of Finance 2010).

Under the reform, municipalities were allowed to levy a municipal property tax in the range of 1.4 to 2.1 per cent on the assessed value of land, buildings and depreciable items such as machinery, equipment, airplanes and vending machines. In addition, prefecture authorities were empowered to levy a property tax on the high-value depreciable assets of large businesses. The tax is levied only on the value greater than what has already been taxed by the municipal property tax. For example, in Tokyo owners of offices have to pay tax on any space beyond a thousand square meters at a rate of 600 yen (around 240 baht) per year.

Capital gains tax is collected on transfers of land, machinery, golf course memberships and other assets. For the most part, the capital gain is taxed through income tax in the regular way. But for any property owned for less than five years, the capital gain is taxed at 9 per cent to discourage speculation, compared to 4–5 per cent otherwise.

France

France has three principal property taxes. Since 1989, wealth tax has been levied on the net value of a household's wealth above 1.3 million euros (53 million baht). In 2007 the tax yielded 442 million euros (18 billion baht) (Mathieu 2008). The tax is levied on property of all kind including houses, land, buildings, jewelry, furniture, cars, airplanes and boats, with exemptions for property used for making a living and items that have high emotional value such as antiques over a hundred years old, art works and historic cars (Public Finances General Directorate 2009). The rate of tax ranges from 0.75 to 1.8 per cent. Taxes are also levied on developed and undeveloped land at rates decided by local government bodies (Public Finances General Directorate 2009).

Proposals for Thailand

For several decades, the Finance Ministry has proposed a draft Land and Buildings Tax Act with a principal aim of promoting better distribution of land ownership and more efficient usage of land. The act has twice received approval from cabinet (during the governments of Chuan Leekpai, 1997–2001, and Abhisit Vejjajiva, 2008–11) but has never been passed into law. The law is framed on the benefit principle that those who benefit from public goods and services should bear the burden of creating them. It is not based on the principle of the ability to pay, and hence is not designed to combat inequality.

As the law aims to collect tax from "everyone" it may face widespread opposition.

Thailand ought to consider wealth taxes along the lines of those in France, South Korea and Japan.

The tax should be levied only on land and buildings, because of the difficulties in assessment and collection in the case of other kinds of wealth. There is already a system for assessing the value of land, and the value of buildings can be assessed independently without allowing discretion to assessing officials. The tax should be levied on gross wealth as computing net wealth will require extra administration in checking debt documents. Moreover, if allowance is made for debt, why not for other management expenses, which will further complicate the calculation. In all the countries studied above except France, gross wealth is used.

As there is a strong possibility of a property tax facing opposition, especially from the urban middle class, the tax should initially be imposed only on those of relatively high wealth, namely on those with total gross value (all over the country) of 20 million baht or more. This figure is chosen as it is the typical price of a house bought by the upper middle class.[3]

As there are no comprehensive data on the value of buildings, it is difficult to analyze the impact of different rate structures. Thailand might follow the progressive rate structures found in Taiwan and South Korea, but initially set the rates low on grounds that this is a new kind of tax. Figure 9.5 presents a putative rate structure: from 20 to 50 million baht at 0.25 per cent; from 50 to 100 million at 0.5 per cent; from 100 to 500 million at 1.5 per cent; and above 500 million at 3 per cent.

Other wealth taxes that may be considered are: a capital gains tax on the increase in value of an assets (such as real estate) at the time of sale;[4] a betterment levy on the increased value (windfall gain) of real estate arising from government investment in infrastructure in the vicinity; and an inheritance tax.

Conclusion

The gains of past economic growth have fallen largely to a small segment of the population, resulting in demands for fiscal policies that promote better distribution of income. This chapter has proposed four strategies for reducing inequality of income and wealth.

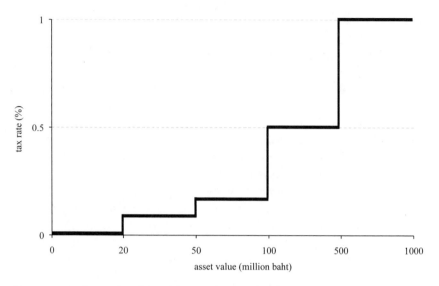

Figure 9.5 Example of Wealth Tax for Thailand

Reform of investment incentives. The current system of investment incentives favors large-scale enterprises, promotes spatial concentration of industry, and deprives the government of large amounts of potential revenue. In addition, the system is highly discriminatory. Incentives given to some amount to burdens for others in the form of higher competition and an increased tax burden. The government should weigh up the comparative benefits of a system that complicates the tax structure for the benefit of a few, as against a simpler and lower tax structure imposed equally on all. The grant of incentives should be limited to individual cases that conform to the development strategy and are of special importance.

Adjustment of income tax allowances and exemptions. The current structure of income tax allowances and exemptions results in those of low income subsidizing those of higher income who are legally able to use loopholes to avoid tax, in contravention of the principles of fairness and ability to pay. The system should be completely overhauled and based on sound principles.

Negative income tax. Negative income tax is a system that combines the tax system and welfare system in order to improve the targeting of government subsidies. Such a system in Thailand will improve the government's information on the low-income population and hence improve the efficiency of government welfare policies. The system is also designed to encourage people to find work, earn more and become more self-reliant, unlike many other welfare schemes. In addition, the system has low operating costs and hence is an efficient way to reduce poverty.

Wealth taxes. Land ownership is highly concentrated and is positively correlated with income (the better off own more land). The current tax structure favors the wealthy. Hence property taxes are an appropriate tool to help overcome poverty, reduce inequality and finance government activities.

Taiwan, South Korea, Japan and France have been successful in raising government revenue from property taxes based on the principle of ability to pay. Thailand should follow their example by levying a progressive tax on holdings of land and buildings above a value of 20 million baht. The current tax on property transfer should also be retained.

In sum, the government should use tax and fiscal tools to reduce inequality and improve the distribution of income and wealth by reforming investment promotion, overhauling the system of tax allowances and exemptions, and introducing a negative income tax and a wealth tax levied on higher-end land and buildings.

Notes

1. The author would like to thank Withi Panichwong and Mayoon Bunyarat of the Fiscal Policy Office for advice and assistance.
2. If a house has been owned for 2 years or more, the rate ranges from 9 to 36 per cent of the capital gain; if owned for 1–2 years, the rate is 40 per cent, and if owned for less than 1 year it is 50 per cent.
3. According to Thai Military Bank (2013), those with income of 200,000 per month can raise a 25-year loan to buy a house valued at 20 million baht.
4. The current income tax on property transfer has the nature of a capital gains tax, but has the problem that it may encourage speculation as the amount of expenses that can be claimed against the tax is high if the property is owned for a short time and decreases the longer the property has been owned.

References

Bahl, R. 2009. *Fixing the Property and Land Tax Regime in Developing Countries, FIAS Workshop on Raising Taxes Through Regulation.* Washington, DC: World Bank.

Case, K.E. 1994. "The Impact of Taxation and Evaluation Practices on the Timing and Efficiency of Land Use." *Journal of Political Economy* 87, 4: 859–68.

Davies, J.B., S. Sandstrom, A. Shorrocks, and E.N. Wolff. 2008. "The World Distribution of Household Wealth." In Discussion Paper No. 2008/03, UNUWIDER.

Friedman, Milton. 1962. *Capitalism and Freedom*. Chicago: University of Chicago Press.

Greenspan, Alan. 2007. *Remarks at the Treasury Conference on U.S. Capital Markets Competitiveness, Georgetown University, 13 March, in Washington, D.C.*

Guevara, M. 1997. "Comments." In *International Seminar on Land Policy and Economic Development Proceedings*. Taoyuan, Taiwan: International Center for Land Policy Studies and Training.

Hale, D. 1985. "The Evolution of the Property Tax: A Study of the Relation between Public Finance and Political History." *Journal of Politics* 47: 382–404.

Ishi, Hiromitsu. 2001. *The Japanese Tax System*. New York: Oxford University Press.

Jansen, K., and C. Khannabha. 2009. "The Fiscal Space of Thailand: An Historical Analysis." In *Fiscal Space, Policy Options for Financing Human Development*, ed. R. Roy and A. Heuty. London: Earthscan, pp. 325–89.

Jones, R.S. 2009. "Reforming the Tax System in Korea to Promote Economic Growth and Cope with Rapid Population Ageing." OECD Economics Department Working Papers No. 671.

Kim, J. 2008. "Tax Policy in Korea: Recent Changes and Key Issues." Paper presented at conference on "Tax Reform in Globalization Era: World Trend and Japan's Choice," Hitotsubashi University.

————. 2005. "Tax Reform Issues in Korea." *Journal of Asian Economics* 16: 973–92.

Li, D. 2006. "U.S. Property Tax Study and Enlightenment to China's Residential Property Tax Reform." MA thesis, University of Nevada, Reno.

Lynn, A. 1967. "Trends in Taxation of Personal Property." In *The Property Tax: Problems and Potentials*, ed. A.G. Buehler. Princeton, NJ: Tax Institute of America.

Mathieu, C. 2008. "France's Wealth Tax: Great Fortune is Faring Well." *l'Humanite in* English, Feb. 25, 2008, available at www.humanitein english.com/spip.php?article843Newspaper.

Ministry of Finance. 2010. *Comprehensive Handbook of Japanese Taxes 2010*. Tokyo: Tax Bureau, Ministry of Finance.

NESDB (National Economic and Social Development Board). 2008. *Raingan kan pramoen khwam yak jon pi 2550* [Report Estimating Poverty, 2007]. Bangkok, NESDB.

————. 2011. *Sathanakan khwam yak jon lae khwam loemlam khong prathet thai pi 2553* [State of Poverty and Inequality in Thailand, 2010]. Bangkok: NESDB.

Netzer, D. 1966. *Economics of the Property Tax: Studies of Government Finance.* Washington, DC: The Brookings Institution.

Nualnoi Treerat. 2013. "Setthi jai bun hae borijak wat..." [Merit-minded Millionaires Flock to Donate to Temples...], available at http://thai publica.org/2013/02/personal-income-tax-structure-14/ [accessed June 30, 2013].

Public Finances General Directorate. 2009. *The French Tax System.* Paris: Ministre de l'Économie des finances et de l'industrie.

Pugh, C. 1997. "Poverty and Progress? Reflections on Housing and Urban Policies in Developing Countries, 1976–1996." *Urban Studies* 34, 10: 1547–59.

Surajit Laksanasut et al. 2010. *Khwam thathai khong nayobai kan khlang: su khwam yangyuen lae kan khayai tua thang setthakit raya yao* [The Challenge of Fiscal Policy for Sustainability and Long-term Economic Growth]. Annual seminar 2010. Bangkok: Bank of Thailand.

Teerana Bhongmakapat. 2006. "Kraiyuth Dhiratayakinant wa duai nayobai sethakit" [Kraiyuth Dhiratayakinant on Economic Policy]. *Matichon,* Oct. 18.

Thai Military Bank. 2013. "Rai dai kap kan phon ban" [Income and mortgages], available at http://www.tmbbank.com/personal/homeloan/home-loan-expert.php [accessed June 24, 2013].

Tsui, S.W. 2006. *Alternative Value Capital Instruments: The Case of Taiwan, Working Paper 06-41.* Atlanta, Georgia: Andrew Young School of Policy Studies, Georgia State University, and Lincoln Institute of Land Policy.

USAID. 2009a. *Best Practices in Fiscal Reform and Economic Governance: Implementing Property Tax Reform.* Available at http://pdf.usaid.gov/ pdf_docs/Pnadw479.pdf [accessed Mar. 29, 2015].

————. 2009b. *Property Tax Reform in Developing and Transition Countries.* Available at http://pdf.usaid.gov/pdf_docs/PNADW480.pdf [accessed Mar. 29, 2015].

Contributors

Chainarong Khrueanuan is lecturer in the Faculty of Politics and Law, Burapha University, Chonburi.

Chaiyon Praditsil is chairperson of the Department of Public Administration at Rambhai Barni Rajabhat University, Chanthaburi.

Chris Baker is an independent scholar.

Dilaka Lathapiphat is an economist at the World Bank.

Duangmanee Laovakul is assistant professor in the Faculty of Economics, Thammasat University.

Nathasit Rakkiattiwong is a researcher at the Thailand Development Research Institute.

Nopanun Wannathepsakul is assistant professor at the Faculty of Economics, Chulalongkorn University.

Nualnoi Treerat is associate professor at the Faculty of Economics, Chulalongkorn University.

Pan Ananapibut is head of Tax Development Section in the Ministry of Finance.

Pasuk Phongpaichit is professor in the Faculty of Economics, Chulalongkorn University.

Parkpume Vanichaka is a PhD student at Waseda University, Tokyo.

Sarinee Achavanuntakul is an independent writer and researcher.

Ukrist Pathmanand is research professor at the Institute of Asian Studies, Chulalongkorn University.

Wanicha Direkudomsak is an economist at the Bank of Thailand.

Index